From the Marine Corps to College

From the Marine Corps to College

*Transitioning from the Service
to Higher Education*

Jillian Ventrone

ROWMAN & LITTLEFIELD
Lanham • Boulder • New York • London

Published by Rowman & Littlefield
A wholly owned subsidiary of The Rowman & Littlefield Publishing Group, Inc.
4501 Forbes Boulevard, Suite 200, Lanham, Maryland 20706
www.rowman.com

16 Carlisle Street, London W1D 3BT, United Kingdom

British Library Cataloguing in Publication Information Available

Library of Congress Cataloging-in-Publication Data

Ventrone, Jillian, 1973–
From the Marine Corps to college : transitioning from the service to higher education / Jillian
Ventrone.
pages cm
Includes bibliographical references and index.
ISBN 978-1-4422-3720-9 (cloth : alk. paper) — ISBN 978-1-4422-3721-6 (electronic)
ISBN 978-0-8108-9521-8 (pbk : alk. paper)
1. Veterans—Education—United States. 2. Marines—Education—United States. 3. United States.
Marine Corps. I. Title.
UB357.V25 2014
378.1'982697—dc23
2014013314

∞™ The paper used in this publication meets the minimum requirements of American
National Standard for Information Sciences Permanence of Paper for Printed Library
Materials, ANSI/NISO Z39.48-1992.

Printed in the United States of America

Contents

Preface

The Iraq and Afghanistan wars have taken a harsh toll on our military's population. Some service members come back from combat ready for a change of pace; others get caught up in the drawdown currently occurring within the services. Many of these service members decide to pursue higher education. Veterans' education benefits are a source of much discussion, but they are often hard to decipher. *From the Marine Corps to College: Transitioning from the Service to Higher Education* aims to simplify this process.

Introduction

From the Marine Corps to College assists active-duty, transitioning service members and their family members in the quest for higher education or vocational training. The educational information in this book will act as a guide through the transition process. While written specifically for Marines, service members from all military branches will find it useful.

After working in veterans' higher education as a counselor for several years, I realized that many service members were unaware of their educational benefits. I found the main problem to be inaccessible information. The Marine Corps has many educational opportunities available for Marines, but the knowledge needs wider dissemination. Since the Corps has been engaged in two simultaneous wars that have taken a massive toll on its population, I can understand how educational benefits could slip through the cracks.

Marines, sailors, and their families need to be able to access the information they need to pursue their educational goals, whether traditional or nontraditional. Unfortunately, if a Marine does not know where to gain the information he requires, he will be left to his own devices. Word of mouth only goes so far to inform a population, and there is much scuttlebutt in the Marine Corps regarding available benefits.

I wrote *From the Marine Corps to College* to rectify this situation. Young Marines who have only recently finished their Military Occupational Specialty (MOS) training and Marines preparing to retire will all benefit from reading this book and learning how to use their available education benefits. I have included stories of Marines I worked with at different points in their careers, but I changed their names and ranks to protect their identities. This enables all readers to gain a more realistic understanding of the transition and higher education process. I also included the extra resources I have found and use on a daily basis in order to facilitate on-the-go knowledge. If a Marine does not receive counseling prior to separation but picks up this book, he will be armed with the necessary knowledge to get started and fund his education.

Many of the Marines I counsel are worried about pursuing higher education. I am always struck by how the thought of school scares them. Battle-hardened Marines afraid of school—how is this possible? At some point, I realized that they are referring to their high school experiences, not knowing that college is completely different. On top of that, after spending a minimum of four years in the Corps, their perspectives are different now; they will be more vested in their education.

If a Marine sets his mind on receiving an education, either traditional or vocational, nothing can stop him. They are the most resilient individuals I have ever met. So many of those I have helped have undergone tremendous stressors, including traumatic brain injuries and loss of limbs, but most persevere.

I work with Marines from all different MOSs, but the vast majority are infantrymen. These Marines are constantly shipped off to war or training, and yet many still manage to pursue higher education while on active duty. I have worked with a staff sergeant who is almost done with his doctoral degree in education; a captain attending an MBA program at the University of California, Los Angeles; a sergeant who was accepted to Columbia University for his bachelor's degree; and a Marine gunner who finished his master's degree and is now a professor as well. If you are on active duty and cannot imagine having the time to start school, think again. Most Marines get started the same way. It can be done as long as you begin at a slow and steady pace.

I hope that if you are a Marine, you will take the time to read this book and pass it along to your friends and spouse. Disseminating the proper information will help every Marine pursue a high-quality education and understand how to fund it using available active-duty and veterans' benefits. If used correctly, the benefits discussed here will help sustain veterans throughout their quest for education and enable them to successfully transition.

Chapter One

Getting Started

Most Marines whom I counsel have a difficult time getting started with higher education. School is a new and foreign environment that they are unsure how to navigate. This chapter will offer students advice pertaining to the steps that must be taken in order to initiate the process.

GETTING STARTED

The most important step in pursuing higher education is simply to begin. That first step is often the most difficult, but once it is taken, everything else will fall into place. This chapter explains the steps to take to get the ball rolling.

If you are on active duty and have no idea how to get started, contact your local education center for guidance. Make an appointment with an academic counselor who will guide you through the process and help tailor your educational pathway to meet your specific needs. Typically, the first step is to attend an education brief through the base education department. For many branches, such as the Marine Corps, this brief is mandatory for first-time active-duty Tuition Assistance (TA) users.

If you are on active duty but preparing to transition, you should also contact the local base education center for an appointment with an academic counselor. The education counselors can help prepare a transition plan for your future educational pursuits. Plus, you can receive guidance pertaining to federal and state-based education benefits.

If you are already separated from the military but near a military base, you can still contact the education center for an appointment. Otherwise, once you find a school, the veterans' representatives should be your first phone call. They can offer guidance that will help you get started.

The following checklist will help you structure an educational plan of attack. Take the time to write down your answers and review the information.

1. What do you want to be when you grow up? (This is still a difficult question for many of the career service members whom I counsel.)
2. What type of school should you attend—traditional or vocational?
3. Do you need a two-year or a four-year institution?
4. Do you have a school picked out already?
5. What are the institution's application requirements?
6. Have you collected your required documents?
7. Have you applied to the institution?
8. How will you pay for your school?

Let's sort through the list to help you start making decisions.

WHAT DO YOU WANT TO BE WHEN YOU GROW UP?

If you know which career you would like to pursue, you are already a few steps ahead. If not, try a self-discovery site such as CareerScope (http://www.gibill.va.gov/studenttools/careerscope/index.html) or O*NET OnLine (http://www.onetonline.org/). Both sites are free and might help narrow down possible career fields to fit one's personality type. Researching different career possibilities, including income levels, job openings, and required education levels, usually helps Marines begin to develop an interest in a specific pathway. (More information on these sites can be found in chapter 3, "Research Tools.")

If you have no idea which career pathway to take, getting started at the local community college is often the best bet. Attending a community college may help you test the waters. Declare for an associate degree in general studies, and use the elective credits to try out different subjects. Elective credits are built into degree plans and offer you freedom to pursue topics outside of the range of your declared major. Many community colleges offer vocational classes; if you think that might also be a viable pathway, you can add some of these classes as well.

WHAT TYPE OF SCHOOL SHOULD YOU ATTEND: TRADITIONAL OR VOCATIONAL?

If you have decided upon a specific career choice, you also need to decide upon the type of school necessary to achieve the appropriate degree or certification. Education that is traditional in nature, such as criminal justice, engineering, business, and the like, will require a traditional degree path at a regionally accredited institution of higher learning.

Education that is vocational in nature may require a nationally accredited vocational school. The different types of schools that you can select for your educational pursuits are discussed in depth later in this book. Always check at your local community college to see if the vocational education you are interested in pursuing is offered. Oftentimes, community colleges have apprenticeship or on-the-job training (OJT) programs attached to their vocational training options.

DO YOU NEED A TWO-YEAR OR FOUR-YEAR INSTITUTION?

Does your educational pathway require a two-year or four-year degree? If in doubt, check O*NET OnLine, or contact the schools in the area and inquire about the level of degree offered for that particular field of study. O*NET demonstrates the different educational levels along with corresponding wages nationally or for a selected state.

Most vocational pathways require either one- or two-year certification, and oftentimes an associate degree might be required. Most career fields that are traditional in nature (think white-collar work) require a four-year bachelor's degree or a graduate-level degree.

DO YOU HAVE A SCHOOL PICKED OUT ALREADY?

If you have a school (or schools) that you are interested in attending, check to see that it is accredited and offers the degree you would like to attain. If so, the very first phone call you make should be to the veterans' representatives, who should be able to answer all of your questions. If not, they will direct you to the appropriate individuals.

Here are a few questions to ask the veterans' representatives:

- What are the admissions requirements? Are they flexible for veterans? Do you need an SAT or ACT? What are the admissions deadlines?
- Will the school accept military transcripts (Joint Services Transcript)?
- Is the institution a member of Servicemembers Opportunity Colleges?
- Which GI Bill is best for the school (Montgomery GI Bill [MGIB] or Post 9/11)?
- Will you have to pay out of pocket for any tuition or fees above and beyond the amount that the GI Bill will cover?
- Does the school approximate how much money books will cost yearly?
- Where are veterans buying their books? Through the bookstore or online? Is there a book exchange or rental program for veterans aboard the campus?
- What veteran services are offered at the institution or nearby?
- How far away is the closest VA center (http://www.va.gov)?
- How many veterans attend the school?
- Does the institution have a student veterans' organization?
- How can you find other veterans who need roommates (if applicable)?

- Does the school have a veterans' center, and what resources are available in the center?
- What helpful hints can they offer pertaining to your attendance at the school?

If you are trying to decide between two schools, hopefully the answers to these questions will offer more guidance.

If you do not know where to go to school, read on for more advice. College Navigator, which is discussed in the "Research Tools" chapter (chapter 3), can be incredibly helpful for conducting school searches. Remember, when in doubt, the local community college is a safe bet, and getting started should be the goal.

If you narrow down your search to a few schools but are still unsure which one to choose, make a quick campus visit, check the application process, and review the timeline restrictions. Oftentimes settling on a school requires a leap of faith, but many small, often overlooked factors can help guide your decision as well. For example, if you are about to deploy and are indecisive about choosing between two different schools, the school that offers the smoothest registration process might be a better choice. Service members have to consider time spent and mission demands since pursuing education while on active duty remains an off-duty benefit.

WHAT ARE THE INSTITUTION'S APPLICATION REQUIREMENTS?

Depending upon the type of school you choose, they might have stringent application requirements, or they might be quite lenient. Application requirements can help you eliminate schools if you missed deadlines or do not possess the materials required for submission—for example, an SAT or ACT score or letters of recommendation.

If you choose a four-year university or college, most likely the institution will require SAT or ACT scores and a formal application process. If you opt for community college, you can avoid a long application process and transfer to a university after acquiring a predetermined amount of college credit. The amount of credit that will be required to finish prior to being eligible for the transfer process will be based upon the transfer requirements of the institution where you are trying to finish your bachelor's degree. If you are pursuing a vocational degree or certificate, these types of schools typically have open admissions similar to community colleges.

If you have a quick transition to go through from active duty, the open admissions process with a local community college can be a less stressful transition into higher education. As long as you follow an appropriate course of study, dictated by an academic counselor at your school, you should not need to worry about the transfer process at a later date. The counselors will tell you which classes you are required to take to be eligible for transfer, and they will be listed on your academic degree or transfer plan.

HAVE YOU COLLECTED ALL REQUIRED DOCUMENTS?

Verify with your school of choice which documents they want from you prior to applying. If an ACT or SAT is required, have you tested? Do you have proof of residency? Have you applied for your GI Bill and received your Certificate of Eligibility (COE)? If you are going to attend a university, you might need a completed application, submitted test scores, letters of recommendation, an application fee, and transcripts. Open admissions institutions such as community colleges and vocational schools usually require a completed online application and proof of payment such as the COE for GI Bill or a TA voucher for active-duty personnel. Visit the "Cost and Payment Resources" chapter of this book (chapter 6) to learn how to apply for your benefits.

HAVE YOU APPLIED TO THE INSTITUTION?

Complete the required application process using all applicable documents. This process is usually online and can take quite a bit of time to go through. Most sites will save your information for a certain number of days if you are unable to finish in one sitting. The "Admissions Process" chapter of this book (chapter 5) will offer more detailed guidance for this area. Many of the Marines I counsel request help with this process, especially since a personal statement essay section often appears in one of the steps.

HOW WILL YOU PAY FOR YOUR SCHOOL?

This is the time to pay good attention to your funding possibilities! When discussing funding options for education, GI Bills are best for veterans and

TA is best for active-duty service members. MGIB and Post 9/11 are not the same. Both help with academic funding, but there are sharp differences in how the two bills work. Veterans who use either bill will find that a great many expenses are still left uncovered.

Active-duty service members and veterans can apply for Federal Student Aid (FSA) for potential extra help. Veterans also have unemployment as an option. Check out your state's Department of Labor for more information regarding unemployment eligibility and possibilities. Many of the active-duty Marines and sailors I work with are awarded Pell Grant money through the Free Application for Federal Student Aid (FAFSA), and Pell Grants do not need to be repaid. The "Cost and Payment Resources" chapter (chapter 6) offers more detailed information about funding your education.

To recap the above checklist in an abbreviated format:

- Choose a career.
- Find a school.
- Organize your finances.

If you are undecided upon a career, get started on general education classes at the local community college. Exercising your brain is never a mistake.

Chapter Two

Which School Is Best for Me?

Finding a school that fits specific needs can be difficult. Plus, the needs of veterans are not the same as the needs of traditional higher education students. Veterans should complete thorough research of their available options before settling on one school. Make sure to pick an institution that offers a comprehensive veteran services department. Having a solid support system in place in case services are needed is a sign that the institution understands the special needs of its veteran population.

Read on for information regarding:

- Active-duty needs
- Veteran needs

WHICH SCHOOL IS BEST FOR ME?

Choosing a college or university is a personal process. Schools are not a dime a dozen. Each institution offers different educational and social experiences. Determining which one best suits your needs will take a bit of research and exploration.

Because higher education institutions come in all shapes and sizes, it is imperative that you prepare appropriately. Identifying your personal needs early on will help eliminate hundreds of schools. If you are unsure of where to begin, start with the basics. Geographic location, setting, size, type, and cost are good determining criteria. Military-based concerns should be addressed on top of these issues. Both active-duty and veteran service members will likely face acculturation issues at some point during their pursuit of higher education. Service members will find that institutions that offer an array of veteran services will be able to provide better support for their needs.

I work with a reconnaissance Marine who gave me great insight into the inner workings of the mind of an infantryman who had difficulty acculturating to his environment. Sergeant Kimball wanted to take classes face-to-face on a college campus. A couple of weeks into one of his classes, he came to speak with me. I could tell when he arrived that he was fit to be tied! He was upset over a situation at school and told me he was going to drop the class. Now, that sounded alarm bells in my head. Apparently the professor had organized the students into groups for a project. Sergeant Kimball had been placed in a group with three female students in their early twenties. During the first group meeting, the young women spent their time discussing how amazing it was to have kids while in high school so their parents could watch them and they could still go out and get drunk.

Well, I was shocked, but not completely knocked off my rocker. Sergeant Kimball was attending school in an affluent area of California known for such television shows as *The Housewives*. Obviously, he did not react well. He explained to me (in vivid detail, I might add) exactly how he felt while he was experiencing the moment.

Let's understand that this particular Marine has experienced many combat deployments and does not have time for ridiculousness in his life. He is also very hardworking and is actively pursuing higher education to better himself. His time is valuable, he wants to spend it wisely, and this experience did not fit the bill. Needless to say, I was not going to let him drop the class. I talked to him about understanding the situation he was in, coping with the environment, and speaking with the professor in private about other options for him.

Dropping classes without exhausting all pathways first is not the best pathway. Oftentimes, professors will be cognizant of their student population, but not always. It is imperative that you use your voice if you find yourself in an uncomfortable situation. Always try discussing your concerns with your professor. Most will understand and try to make accommodations. If that pathway does not work, try talking to your academic counselor. This is why it is imperative that schools with significant veteran populations maintain veteran-only academic counselors. These individuals understand service members' special needs and also understand how to help in situations such as this one.

With the understanding that active-duty and veteran service members have very different needs, it is best to prepare accordingly. If you are transitioning from active duty, make a list of any new concerns you think might be relevant to a veteran before choosing your new school. This may help with the selection or elimination process.

Active-duty service members might want to consider issues such as a school's ability to remain flexible with military students for times when deployments and Permanent Change of Station (PCS) moves arise, credit transfer possibilities, degree availability, online options, flexible classroom offerings, and contact ability. Veterans may want to consider a school's location, face-to-face class availability for the full housing allowance on the Post 9/11 GI Bill, veterans' department for support, degree options, campus services, transition services, and veteran population. Both active-duty and veteran service members should also take into account a school's policy toward prior learning credit. Schools that place value on a service member's military training are helping you invest in your future.

Be skeptical of schools that offer promises that seem too good to be true. If the promises do not hold, you could find yourself in troubled waters. Many less-than-reputable institutions claim that they maintain high job placement percentages, but students find out later that the numbers were manipulated. Other institutions state that credits from their schools are highly transferable, but students later learn that they have wasted their time and hard-earned GI Bill benefits after it is too late. College is hard work, and it takes hard work to get to graduation. Any institution that promises you that life will be easy as pie causes me great alarm.

ACTIVE-DUTY NEEDS

Many active-duty Marines do not have enough time left in service to finish an associate or bachelor's degree before separation, but would like to start working toward their education. Several options should be considered before moving forward.

Credit transferability should be at the top of the high-priority list. Transferability is a sticky topic. Ultimately, credit acceptance is up to the final institution. Schools usually consider the accreditation of the prior institution and specific program requirements when reviewing transfer credit.

Classes do not always transfer for credit they were originally intended to fill. You must also keep an eye on how many credits an institution will accept. For example, Arizona State University (ASU) will transfer a maximum of 64 lower-division semester hours (i.e., 100- and 200-level classes) from a regionally accredited community college (https://transfer.asu.edu/credits), although some exceptions apply for veterans. If you intend on transferring to ASU to complete a bachelor's degree, taking more than 64 lower-division credits from the school you are currently attending would be unproductive. Try your best not to find yourself in a situation where credits will not transfer or might need to be repeated.

Consider a few points before moving forward in this situation:

1. Always check the institution's accreditation. I cannot emphasize this point enough. Chapter 4 in this book reviews the different types of accreditation and concerns to be aware of prior to selecting an institution. If you make the wrong choice, you might be backtracking later on. I once worked with a Marine who had to backtrack after completing two years of school because he chose an institution that did not have the right type of accreditation necessary for his preferred field.

2. Consider the state you come from or intend to move to before choosing a school to attend. Many schools have satellite locations in other states or aboard military installations. If you can find one from your state, in most cases it will be better for your needs. For example, if you are a Texas resident, intend to return to Texas, and are stationed aboard Camp Pendleton, try Central Texas College (CTC). CTC is a Texas state community college operating aboard the base. It is highly unlikely that you will lose any credit upon your transfer to a Texas state university, but there is still no guarantee.

3. If you know which institution you would like to attend after separation from the military, see if the school offers online classes. If feasible, it would be best to start while on active duty at the school where you intend to finish when you are a veteran. Many schools, including state-based two-year and four-year institutions, offer online classes and are approved for Tuition Assistance (TA). Colorado State University, Penn State, and the University of Maryland are a few of the big four-year universities with fully online bachelor's degrees that are TA approved. Many community colleges offer fully online associate degrees, such as Saddleback College, just north of Camp Pendleton; Northern Virginia Community College (NOVA), near Quantico Marine Corps Base; and Central Texas Community College, which is located aboard several military installations. Check the Department of Defense Memorandum of Understanding website (www.dodmou. com) to see if your school is approved for TA. Attending a school online that you can continue to attend once separated will make your transition much easier—plus you will not run the risk of losing credits during the transfer process.

4. If these options are not possible, contact the school you are interested in attending upon separation, and ask if they have transfer agreements with any particular schools. Most big universities are fed by local community colleges, and most community colleges offer online classes. Usually, all big state universities have transfer agreements with the local state community colleges. This is typically the safest pathway to pursue.

5. Check with the local education center to see which schools have a presence aboard the base.

The College Navigator site (http://nces.ed.gov/collegenavigator/), which will be covered fully in chapter 3 ("Research Tools"), is a useful tool if you are unaware of schools located back home.

Degree availability is a concern. Most Marines need to go to school online because of job demands. Online degree availability is not typically as broad as in a traditional setting. Sometimes specific degrees must be done in a face-to-face environment. For example, most engineering and kinesiology degrees require on-campus coursework.

When researching a school, check to see that it maintains the flexible classroom offerings you need to be successful. Does the institution offer weekend, evening, or hybrid classes? Does it offer classes aboard your base? What are the professors' contact policies regarding their active-duty students? Lastly, what can the school offer in the way of support services?

Maybe you intend to study mechanical engineering upon leaving active duty. Although job demands might keep you from pursuing a degree-specific program while on active duty, find a school that meets the general education demands and higher-level math requirements of the school you anticipate attending after your EAS (end of active service).

If you cannot find the degree you want in an online setting, try to complete as many of the required credits, such as the general education classes, without getting into degree-specific classes until you separate from the military. Otherwise, you might have to wait until you are at a new duty station and can find a school that offers the degree nearby. This problem is difficult to work around. Job demands and duty location are sometimes insurmountable.

I bring up the topic of contact concerns with your school, because many Marines simply cannot find their academic counselors at a later date. Unforeseen issues can inadvertently pop up with active-duty service members, like temporary additional duty (TAD) orders and deployments. Hopefully, you have chosen a school that supplies open and constant communication in case any problems arise.

Many schools have clear policies in regard to deployments and may even allow students to finish courses remotely. Institutions with academic counselors strictly for active-duty military and veterans may be able to provide more tailored help. At a minimum, they can give an active-duty service member a clear chain of command to contact when in need of assistance.

If you are an active-duty Marine who is interested in pursuing school to become an officer, you have a couple of pathways. The Marine Corps Enlisted Commissioning Education Program (MECEP) and the Enlisted Commissioning Program (ECP) are the two pathways available while remaining on active duty. Both require checking the current applicable Marine Administrative Messages (MARADMINs) to determine eligibility and requirements.

MECEP currently requires Marines to complete three credits of English, three credits in math or science, and six other credits prior to becoming eligible for the program. MECEP applicants must have a minimum of three years on active duty completed and be at least a sergeant. Individuals accepted into the program must attend a Naval Reserve Officers Training Corps

(NROTC) participating school or a cross-town affiliate. ECP requires the applicant to already possess a bachelor of arts or a bachelor of science degree from an accredited university or college. ECP applicants must have at least one year on active duty completed and at least one year left on contract.

While these are the current educational requirements, always make sure to check the current MARADMINs for up-to-date information. Age restrictions and many other rules apply as well. Request help from your education officer, and visit your local education center to get started on the educational portion of your pathway to becoming an officer.

VETERANS' NEEDS

Veterans' educational needs have been the topic of much discussion. The Post 9/11 GI Bill has allowed today's veterans more flexibility in their educations than ever before, and schools across the country have had significant increases in their veteran student populations. Unfortunately, veterans of the current conflicts face transition issues that pose many difficult challenges. Schools that recognize these challenges and tailor services aboard the campus to meet the special needs of their veteran populations should be recognized for their support.

Be careful when choosing a school that claims it is veteran friendly. A study conducted by the Center for American Progress determined that the criteria for listing schools as "veteran friendly" on some websites and media outlets are unclear. Schools should offer you a proper academic pathway as well as veteran-based support. Be leery of any institution that claims it is "veteran friendly" and cannot back it up with concrete proof.[1]

Ask about campus support services for veterans. You should look for veteran-only academic counselors, VA services on the campus or nearby, nonprofit veteran assistance such as American Veterans (AMVETS) or Disabled American Veterans (DAV), student veteran organizations such as the Student Veterans of America (SVA), financial aid support, unemployment support, contact with off-campus services that specialize in veteran outreach, and a significant student veterans center that is consistently staffed. The center should be prepared to handle, or refer to the appropriate agencies, any problem that comes its way, including, but not limited to, combat-related stress.

Many institutions even offer peer-to-peer mentoring. Saddleback College in Mission Viejo, California, has a peer-mentoring program that may end in a small scholarship for the mentor. The scholarship has rigorous qualifications for acceptance. The application requires that several essays be submitted for acceptance and again after completion in order to receive the award. The program enables new veteran students and those who have attended the institution for a while to intermingle. This interaction will boost the confidence of the incoming veteran and provide him or her with a support system, while enabling the veteran mentor to give back to the community.

Many great academic institutions host the Veterans Upward Bound (VUB) program aboard their campuses, including ASU (https://eoss.asu.edu/trio/vub). The VUB program is designed to encourage and assist veterans in their pursuit of higher education. The federally funded program aims to increase and improve qualified veterans' English, math, computer (to assist with literacy), laboratory science, foreign language, and college-planning skills. All of the courses are free, and ASU offers courses daily on three of the school's campuses. One campus has classes offered at three different times during the day to better meet the schedules of the veteran population. Check the national VUB program website (http://www.navub.org/) to find out if your school offers the program.

Other schools provide their staff training programs such as Vet Net Ally. Vet Net Ally was designed by a former Marine who is currently the director of veterans' services at California State University, Long Beach. Vet Net Ally creates awareness for veteran-related concerns and teaches individuals involved in higher education how to properly assist veterans who approach them for assistance, oftentimes with confidential concerns.

School location is important for veterans for many factors other than the Monthly Housing Allowance (MHA) attached to Post 9/11. Try to find a school that is within a decent driving distance. Usually, in a traditional educational environment, we live where we go to school. This may not be the case for many veterans. Often, veterans are older and have families they must support while they pursue higher education. Sometimes jobs dictate where we can live, and driving long distances to get to class may add unneeded stress to an already stressful transition. Check for veteran services offered around the school, because if you need help, you may not want to drive a hundred miles to get it.

The setting of the school's location is also important. If you need to be in a city for nightlife or a more fast-paced lifestyle, you should take that into consideration. If you prefer something without many distractions, consider a quieter institution in a smaller town location. You can also check to see if the veterans' center at the school has a designated veteran-only study space allocated for quiet study time.

Class availability is imperative for veterans for reasons such as MHA amounts under Post 9/11 and socialization. Both of these subjects are vastly different in nature, but extremely important to consider when thinking about your transition to school. The MHA and degree plan requirements under Post 9/11 are addressed in the "Cost and Payment Resources" chapter (chapter 6).

Socialization is sometimes an issue that doesn't become a concern until several months after separation. While I am not writing this book to depress my readers regarding some of the issues facing the veteran population, I do want to remind you of a few things to consider.

Isolation can become a concern for transitioning veterans who face an unknown civilian population that doesn't operate in the same regimented fashion they are used to in the military. Marines who isolate themselves run a great risk of facing difficulty in the transition process. Making contact and developing relationships with other veterans at the school are good ways to combat this issue.

Marines should review the following checklist with a veterans' representative at the school they plan on attending:

1. Make contact so you have a face to connect with the name.
2. Explain your situation, and ask for helpful hints for anything you may need.
3. Ask about housing and where you can find other veterans for roommates.
4. Find out what services the school has set in place for its veteran population. Maybe the school has a veteran-only student body (president, vice president, secretary, etc.) that helps plan social events or promotes veteran well-being at the institution.
5. Determine where the closest VA center is located.
6. Ask about student veteran organizations (like SVA) available aboard the campus.
7. Find out about the institution's veteran population. How many veteran students attend the school? Does the school or vet center host any veteran-only events?
8. Do veterans receive early admission?
9. Is there a veterans' academic counselor?
10. Is the institution a Servicemembers Opportunity College (SOC)?

Veteran interaction aboard the campus is important for veteran success. Many veteran departments at schools actively participate in community events involving veterans. This is a great way to meet new friends and help your peers. Interaction is not solely for you to create a school support web and make friends. Networking with other veterans is a great way to keep in touch with other people who have shared similar experiences. Sharing experiences with those who have "been there, done that" may help you reintegrate into civilian life faster. This network can also be an amazing tool for job searches and entrepreneurship possibilities at a later date.

Researching the above-mentioned topics may help you understand the school's overall culture and attitude toward its veteran population. If the school does not seem to have many veteran services set in place, you may want to consider other options. Schools should provide veterans a multitude of support services in case they face unforeseen issues while transitioning and need help.

The VA recognized the need for veterans to hear transition troubles and successes from peers and created a website to help. Make the Connection (http://maketheconnection.net/) helps veterans through shared experiences and support services. The site contains resources and videos from veterans who have faced issues you may be facing and offers advice based on personal experience.

Chapter Three

Research Tools

You now have a better idea of your potential academic needs whether on active duty or already a veteran. Conducting meaningful research is the next step. Research tools are important resources to help you make more informed decisions regarding education. If you have no idea what you want to be when you grow up, this section offers free tools that assist in career exploration. CareerScope (through the VA), O*NET OnLine, and the Defense Activity for Non-Traditional Education Support's (DANTES) Kuder Journeys offer users possible career matches for specific personality types and a sneak peek into different career fields. College Navigator is a wonderful tool to help users find schools through broad and narrow search options.

The following websites will be discussed:

- College Navigator/O*NET OnLine
- Kuder Journeys
- CareerScope/My Next Move for Veterans (VA)
- VA Chapter 36 (counseling services)
- Know Before You Enroll

COLLEGE NAVIGATOR AND O*NET ONLINE

http://nces.ed.gov/collegenavigator/
http://www.onetonline.org/

College Navigator and O*NET OnLine are go-to websites for transitioning Marines. Both are quick, efficient, free, and easy to use. College Navigator will help you begin sifting through school options. O*NET OnLine will give you career-based background information to follow up with your degree decision.

College Navigator, a comparison tool offered through the National Center for Education Statistics, is a solid starting point for college or vocational school searches. Refined search options, side-by-side evaluations, interactive maps, saved searches, and spreadsheet printouts enable users to conduct effective searches for schools, whether vocational or traditional in nature.

Begin searching based on the ZIP code of your desired residence. The ZIP code search allows exploration of institutions from a 5- to a 250-mile radius, which throws down a broad range of institutions to peruse. Refine the search to narrow the results. Searching by institution type, including public or private status, two- or four-year degree offerings, levels of awards offered, tuition and fees, and campus setting, will result in more advanced choices.

After an initial search, the schools that matched the selected criteria will pop up in a list. The list shows the city and distance from the listed ZIP code. Click on a school to see more detailed information, such as tuition costs, enrollment, admissions criteria, retention and graduation rates, programs, and accreditation.

For example, you could search based on the following criteria:

- 60660 ZIP code for Chicago
- Fifty-mile radius
- Public and private, not-for-profit school
- Bachelor's degrees
- Campus setting: city
- Browse for programs: Communication and journalism

The next step is to begin sifting through the schools listed. All school information should be reviewed. If you click on a private school and tuition is listed at $40,000, further research must be conducted to determine if the school is financially viable for you, since the GI Bill limits funds available for private institutions. If the graduation rates are 10 percent, you might wonder why they are so low. Maybe you should consider an institution with a more solid graduation track record.

O*NET OnLine is a great follow-up site for College Navigator. O*NET can be used for school searches, but I do not find it detailed enough. The site does not allow users to refine their searches in any detail, such as by making them ZIP code specific. Basically, users can only search by program and state location. However, the site does excel at producing career information related to a particular field of study and is an effective quick reference tool.

If you would like to know information related to a career in your field of study, visit the O*NET OnLine website and type in a career under the link at the top right: "Occupation Quick Search." The site will list all occupations found within the search. This quick, initial search is a great way to find other careers related to the one you were initially interested in, thereby broadening your potential options.

Choosing one of the career options gives users information related to the skills one might need within the career field, as well as the career's work activities and context. Further searching allows users to see educational demands, state-based wages, hiring trends, projected growth, and sometimes even videos demonstrating the careers.

If you are trying to put together a résumé, O*NET is a definite go-to site. The wealth of information regarding most careers can be used to demonstrate deep knowledge. But Marines and sailors also have résumé-writing services offered aboard the main bases for free. Contact your local Transition Assistance Program (TAP) for more information.

DANTES COLLEGE & CAREER PLANNING COUNSELING SERVICES, POWERED BY KUDER® JOURNEY™

http://www.dantes.kuder.com/

DANTES College & Career Planning Counseling Services is a free Internet-based tool designed to aid active-duty and veteran military personnel in exploring potential education and career pathways. The site offers a personality-career assessment, occupational information, education and financial aid information, job search tools, job search engines, and a portfolio section.

The "Assessment" section hosts a personality test to narrow down potential careers. The test results may assist users in determining an appropriate college major and/or career goals. The recommended career list also shows if the pathway has a bright outlook for job growth and if it is considered to be a green economy field.

The "Occupations" section is geared to help users find careers related to the outcome of their personality assessments. This section also enables users to search occupations related to their Military Occupational Specialty (MOS) or previous job experience.

The "Education and Financial Aid" section offers sections that enable users to search for the educational attainment level required for a favorite occupation, complete a school search, learn about and search for financial aid, and search for apprenticeship opportunities. Users are able to save conducted searches.

The "Job Search Tools" section helps users create a résumé, write a cover letter, collect references, and manage all documents with a portfolio. This section offers interview objectives, social networking advice, and career fair searches.

CAREERSCOPE® AND MY NEXT MOVE FOR VETERANS

http://www.gibill.va.gov/studenttools/careerscope/index.html
http://www.mynextmove.org/vets/

CareerScope® is an interest and aptitude assessment tool offered for free through the VA to eligible benefit recipients. Like Kuder, this site assists Marines in finding the best transition path for different careers depending upon their interests. Marines can pursue information based on the level of college already attained, and the career pathway already determined (or not determined).

My Next Move for Veterans (http://www.mynextmove.org/vets/) is a partnership with O*NET OnLine. Active-duty and veteran service members can search careers similar to their military MOS, specific fields, or industry. The site lists information on career fields that also have registered apprenticeship programs available and enables state-based searches for the programs listed. Bright outlook and green career fields are identified.

Clicking on a specific career option will lead to more information, such as related fields, job duties and activities, and required knowledge and skills. My Next Move for Veterans also demonstrates which personality types fit particular fields, technology that might be used or useful to understand, the typical educational level attained in the field, and salary standards. Job and school information is broken down by state.

O*NET also has a career interest profile assessment that can be accessed by selecting "O*NET Interest Profiler" in the lower right-hand corner of the main page.

VA CHAPTER 36 EDUCATIONAL AND VOCATIONAL COUNSELING

http://www.gibill.va.gov/support/counseling_services/

The VA offers free education and career counseling for eligible veterans. Services are intended to help participants facilitate career decisions, choose appropriate career fields and programs of education, and correct any academic or adjustment concerns that may hinder success. Topics of discussion may include subjects such as financial aid options, employment plans, and exploration of career and education objectives.

Eligible veterans:

- Are eligible for VA education benefits (or dependents using transferred benefits) through one of the following chapters: Chapters 30, 31, 32, 33, 35, 1606, or 1607
- Received an honorable discharge not longer than one year earlier
- Have no more than six months remaining on active duty

To receive counseling, eligible participants must correctly fill out an application and return it. The application can be found online (see http://www.vba.va.gov/pubs/forms/VBA-28-8832-ARE.pdf).

This is a particularly good program for Marines already separated from active duty who are not located near an education center on a military base.

KNOW BEFORE YOU ENROLL

The Know Before You Enroll (http://www.knowbeforeyouenroll.org) campaign was originally created by the City of New York (NYC) to give applicable guidance to individuals interested in pursuing higher education. Through a partnership with NYC's program, Know Before You Enroll for Veterans was founded.

Operated by a small nonprofit, Iraq and Afghanistan Veterans of America (IAVA), Student Veterans of America (SVA), the University of San Diego, and Scholarship America, Know Before You Enroll for Veterans offers important information that arms prospective veteran students with the knowledge they need in order to make well-informed school choices. Veterans who are able to make good choices are less likely to find themselves enrolled in less-than-standard institutions.

Unfortunately, the Post 9/11 GI Bill is alluring to some schools that may deliver substandard educations and may not provide adequate support systems for returning veterans. The "Top 10 Tips" section of the website (http://knowbeforeyouenroll.org/top-ten-tips/) offers invaluable information for active-duty and veteran students trying to decide on a school. Two of the tips stood out in my mind as important factors to consider prior to making a final school selection:

1. Never sign anything you do not understand.
2. Ask for the school's cancellation policy in writing.

I often discuss these two issues during counseling appointments. These two questions are not usually foremost in an individual's mind when choosing an institution of higher learning, but both are incredibly important.

If you are concerned about a school's particular enrollment agreement or cancellation policy, you can contact the University of San Diego's Veterans' Legal Clinic (http://www.sandiego.edu/veteransclinic/). The free clinic can review your enrollment agreement and offer advice based on the results.

A few more sites worth mentioning:

- U.S. Department of Education College Affordability and Transparency Center: http://collegecost.ed.gov/
- U.S. Department of Labor's career search tool: http://www.mynextmove.org/
- Bureau of Labor Statistics Occupational Outlook Handbook: http://www.bls.gov/ooh/

Each one of these sites offers a wealth of information pertaining to college costs, career searches, and occupational information, including the necessary level of education and pay associated with the work.

Chapter Four

What Should I Look for in a School?

Within this chapter, four important factors will be discussed that should be considered prior to committing to an institution:

- Types of schools
- School accreditation
- Admissions requirements (including the Leadership Scholar Program)
- Military Awareness: Servicemembers Opportunity Colleges (SOC) and the SOCMAR (SOC Marine Corps Agreement)

Cost should not be eliminated as an important factor because of the parameters of the GI Bills and will be discussed in chapter 5.

TYPES OF SCHOOLS

Now you know how to conduct research, but what are you looking for during your search? Understanding the differences between the types of schools will assist you in your work. Career choice dictates most educational pathways. For example, are you taking a vocational or traditional pathway? Do you need a two-year degree or a four-year degree? If two years are sufficient, then you can eliminate most four-year universities from your search. Narrowing your search down by a few key factors will help in the selection process.

Understanding the options for higher education will enable you to choose the appropriate school for your educational pathway. Technical schools, community colleges, universities, and public and private not-for-profit and for-profit schools have different guiding factors and structures. This section offers brief explanations of the types of schools and how to choose the one that best suits your needs.

Two-Year Schools

Two-year schools are community colleges (CCs) or technical schools. Most are state based, but not always. CCs offer the following:

- Associate degrees
- Transfer pathways to universities and colleges
- Certificate programs
- Vocational programs
- Open enrollment, which is especially good if you had trouble with your high school GPA
- No SAT, ACT, or essay required
- Significantly cheaper tuition and fees compared to universities and colleges

Students who are on a budget can start at a two-year community college before transferring to a university and save a tremendous amount of money. Since community colleges are usually found in numerous locations throughout each state, they are easy to find and often close by your home. The open enrollment policy makes for a stress-free transition from active duty and is the fastest way to start school. Most of the Marines I assist opt for a community college when they are on a time crunch because of deployments or training. Sometimes it is the only pathway, especially if university admission deadline dates have passed. This often happens to Marines deployed to Afghanistan or a Marine Expeditionary Unit (MEU) and to Marines stationed overseas.

Most CCs offer vocational programs that require an associate degree or a certification process. Attending a vocational program at a state CC gives you safe, regionally accredited transfer credit if you would ever like to pursue a bachelor's degree at another regionally accredited school at a later date.

Always check with the specific school about the program you would like to attend. Oftentimes, programs such as nursing are impacted. This means that there are more students than spots available and acceptance may be delayed.

Community colleges frequently offer internships and apprenticeships within the surrounding community. These programs may help you gain employment at a faster rate, generate work experience for a résumé, or qualify you for a specific career.

Four-Year Schools

Four-year schools are colleges or universities. Each state has a state university system, but not all colleges and universities are state based, as you will read about in the next few paragraphs. Four-year schools are characterized by the following:

- They offer bachelor's, master's, MD, and PhD degrees
- Many are research based
- Depending on type of school, they can be expensive
- Many offer on- and off-campus enrichment opportunities, such as study abroad and guest lecture series
- Students obtain degrees that offer a wide range of job opportunities
- There is a broader range of course selection than in community colleges
- State universities have large, diverse campuses and populations; liberal arts colleges have smaller campuses and smaller, more familiar class sizes
- Competitive admissions process

Universities can sometimes be overwhelming to attend. Classes can get so large that you never have a one-on-one conversation with your professor, which can make students feel anonymous. Finding your niche might take some time in a large population, but it will afford you more opportunities to interact. Large institutions usually have numerous degrees and classes to choose from, but smaller liberal arts colleges may be a bit more specialized.

Many students start at their local community college, then they finish their junior and senior years at a university or college. This is an easy pathway to pursue if you are running short on time to prepare, feel like you need more individualized attention at the start of your education, do not want to take the SAT or ACT, or simply have not been to school in a long time and feel safer in a smaller, less competitive environment. Whatever the case, arm yourself with information before making a decision. Sometimes a visit to the campus will settle the issue as well. The school should be a comfortable fit, since you will be spending so much time attending.

Study abroad is always a fun option. Many Marines and sailors opt for school overseas. I met a sailor who went to medical school in the Netherlands, a Marine Corps sergeant who was attending university in Australia, and a corporal who was attending an institution in Canada.

Preparing correctly for study abroad takes some time. Most foreign schools do not abide by the regional accreditation that is preferred for traditional education in the United States. This can cause problems down the road. Make sure to find out if the degree can be translated in the United States prior to committing to attending a foreign institution. Information on foreign degree or credit evaluation can be found on the National Association of Credential Evaluation Services (NACES®) website (http://www.naces.org/). If the degree from the foreign institution you are considering attending cannot be evaluated by our standards, you may have difficulty later on. You run the risk of a potential employer not valuing your degree or a master's degree program not recognizing the level of education you have achieved.

Public Schools (Universities and Community Colleges)

Public schools, often referred to as "state schools," are typically funded by state and local governments. In-state residents receive lower tuition charges than out-of-state residents. Some schools' out-of-state tuition charges can total an extra $10,000 or more per academic year. Sometimes state schools have reciprocal agreements with schools in other states that allow for reduced out-of-state tuition charges—for example, the Midwest Student Exchange Program (MSEP; http://msep.mhec.org/). MSEP is based out of the Midwest and has nine participating states with public schools that charge undergraduate students a maximum of 150 percent of the in-state tuition charges and private schools that offer a 10 percent reduction in tuition.

State schools offer a wide range of classes, degree options, and degree levels, with state residents getting priority admissions. Class size at state schools can be a concern. Sometimes a lecture class can have as many as 250 students enrolled. This can make it difficult to interact with professors or staff.

Each state usually has a flagship university with smaller locations available throughout the state for easier access. In some instances, students attending state universities cannot graduate in the standard four-year timeframe because mandatory classes are full.

Private Schools

Private schools do not receive funding from state or local government. They are financially supported by tuition costs, donations, and endowments. They may be nonprofit or for-profit in nature, and traditional or nontraditional in nature. Private schools usually charge students the same price whether they are in-state or out-of-state residents. Often the cost of private school tuition is more than resident tuition at a state school, but not always. Many private schools offer scholarships and grants to greatly reduce the tuition costs. Usually, private schools have smaller class sizes than public schools, which can mean greater access to professors. Private school acceptance may be less competitive than state acceptance, but not if discussing top-tier or Ivy League institutions. Some private schools have religious affiliations, are historically black or Hispanic-serving institutions, or are single-sex institutions.

For-Profit Institutions

The difference between for-profit and not-for-profit is basically in the title. For-profit schools are operated by businesses, are revenue based, and have to account for profits and losses. According to a recent government report on for-profit schools, the "financial performance of these companies is closely tracked by analysts and by investors," which means that the bottom line is always revenue.[1]

For-profit schools typically have open enrollment. Open enrollment can be helpful when you are transitioning from the military and have many other urgent needs at the same time. Open enrollment means that everyone gains entry to the school. That may prove disastrous for an individual who is not ready for the demands of higher education, but if the student is well prepared, it might provide a good pathway.

If you are looking for ease in the transition process and flexible class start dates, for-profit schools can offer you that benefit. Usually, they have classes starting every eight weeks, or every first Monday of the month, with rolling start dates.

Be informed when choosing your school. The College Board reported average costs of published state school tuition and fees for 2012 at $8,660, and average private school tuition and fees at $29,060. [2]

The for-profit institutions have come under fire recently by Congress for several different concerns, including their intake of Federal Student Aid (FSA) and GI Bill money. If you would like more information on these concerns, try the following two websites:

http://www.harkin.senate.gov/help/forprofitcolleges.cfm
http://www.sandiego.edu/veteransclinic/news_research.php

Veterans should be concerned about private school cost, given that the average cost of private school listed for 2012 was significantly higher than the Post 9/11 payout of $19,198.31 for the academic year 2013–2014. If you decide on a private school that charges tuition and fees above and beyond the Post 9/11 payout amount, check to see whether the school is participating in the Yellow Ribbon Program (YRP). The YRP, which is explained in depth in chapter 6, "Cost and Payment Resources," may help you close the tuition gap.

Not-for-Profit Institutions

According to the National Association of Independent Colleges and Universities, "private, not-for-profit higher education institutions['] purposes are to offer diverse, affordable, personal, involved, flexible, and successful educations to their students." [3]

Not-for-profit private schools can sometimes offer flexible admissions for veterans that many state institutions may not be able to offer. Offering flexible admissions to veterans is a school-specific benefit, and veterans should address the option with their preferred institution.

Private, not-for-profit schools can have tremendous name recognition, like Harvard and Yale University. On a smaller scale, many private, not-for-profit colleges and universities are well known within our own communities. For example, in my hometown of Chicago, Illinois, three well-known private, not-for-profit schools are DePaul University, Loyola University, and

Columbia College. All three of these schools enjoy excellent reputations and are well known throughout the Midwest.

Attending this type of school is typically a safe pathway, especially when listing your school on a résumé. Be aware that private schools can be very expensive, and the cost can sometimes be prohibitive. For example, DePaul is roughly $34,000 per academic year.

The good news is that many private schools also participate in the YRP. For example, DePaul participates with unlimited spots and $12,500. As you will read in chapter 6, which addresses the YRP, this means the VA matches that amount, and you end up with an extra $25,000 on top of your private school maximum of $19,198.31. Basically, your tuition is covered. Make sure to determine if the school is participating in the YRP (and in what manner) before committing to attending.

Vocational-Technical and Career Colleges

Vocational-technical (votech) schools and career colleges prepare students for skill-based careers in technical fields. Many technical schools are state-run, subsidized, and regionally accredited. Credits from these schools are generally accepted elsewhere. Career colleges are private, usually for-profit institutions, and they mostly hold national accreditation. Credits from these schools may not be widely transferable.

Programs at these schools can run anywhere from ten months to four years, depending on the skills required to finish training. Many have rolling admissions. Programs often run year-round, including the summers, in order to get students into the workforce faster.

Typically, in a votech-based program, general education classes such as English and math are not necessary. Program completion results in a certificate of completion or an associate degree in applied science. The associate in applied science will require entry-level math and English classes. Votech schools focus directly on the task at hand, meaning training in a need-based skill and preparing students for a career.

If you have decided to attend a votech pathway, research the school's cost, credentials, faculty, program requirements, and student body prior to committing to a specific institution. Cost is important, since the GI Bill has a set maximum amount it will pay for private school. Find out if you will also be eligible to apply for FSA, but remember that you are mainly interested in the Pell Grant; you can find more information regarding the aid in the "Cost and Payment Resources" chapter (chapter 6).

Determine if the school is licensed by the state and which accreditation it holds. Ask about the professors' backgrounds and qualifications. Find out if you will be able to apply any military credit toward the program and if the program includes on-the-job training or internship possibilities.

Visit the campus to determine what type of equipment you will be trained on and review the faculty setting. Check the school's completion rates, meaning how many students graduate and whether they accomplish this on time. Lastly, verify that the school offers job placement services. Find out the following:

- What is their rate of placement?
- Where are students being placed?
- What positions are they getting right out of school?
- How much money are they earning?

Usually, a phone call and follow-up school visit are required to fully understand the program benefits. Remember that vocational fields prepare students for specific career pathways, and transitioning to a different pathway at a later date will require retraining.

Votech schools usually hold national accreditation. In the following portion of this chapter, I explain the difference between regional and national accreditation. Make note that nationally accredited programs' credits cannot transfer into a regionally accredited school, although some exceptions exist at schools that hold dual accreditation. For this reason, always check the local community college for similar programs. Many community colleges offer vocational programs that can be converted to transferable college credit at a later date.

ACCREDITATION

At this point, you have conducted research and might now have a better idea of a possible future career. You are also armed with the tools you will need in order to search for a school and understand the differences between the types of schools. But what should you be looking for in an institution besides veteran support and degree type? Accreditation should be number one on your list of important factors. Attending a school that is not accredited or does not have the proper accreditation for your career pathway could mean significant problems later on.

The United States does not have a formal federal authority that oversees higher education. Each individual state exercises some level of regulation, but, generally speaking, colleges and universities have the ability to self-govern. Accreditation was created in order to supervise and guide institutions of higher learning in order to assure students that they were receiving valuable educations.

Institutional accreditation means that the college or university as a whole is accredited. This enables the entire school to maintain credibility as a higher learning institution. Only regional or national accrediting agencies can give institutional accreditation.

Accredited schools adhere to the accrediting bodies' standards. Having accreditation is like having quality control for higher education. When searching for schools, accreditation should be an important factor to consider. Students who attend accredited universities and colleges have a greater chance of receiving a quality education and receiving recognition for their degrees.

If a school does not hold an accreditation, you will most likely not be able to apply for federal or state-based financial aid. Credit hours earned from non-accredited schools will not usually transfer into accredited institutions and will not be recognized for entrance into most master's degree programs.

Always look for regional and national accreditation. Before deciding which type is best for you, think about the type of education you are pursuing. If you are pursuing education that is traditional in nature, look for regional accreditation. Traditional education typically prepares students to complete bachelor's degrees and to pursue advanced degrees. Examples of degrees that are considered traditional encompass such subjects as criminal justice, education, engineering, and business. Regional accreditation is the most widely recognized and transferable (credit hours) accreditation in this country. All state (public) schools hold regional accreditation.

There are six regional accrediting bodies in the United States. The accrediting bodies are based on the region of the country:

- Middle States Association of Colleges and Schools: http://www.msche.org/
- New England Association of Schools and Colleges: http://cihe.neasc.org/
- North Central Association of Colleges and Schools: http://www.ncahlc.org/

- Northwest Commission on Colleges and Universities: http://www.nwccu.org/
- Southern Association of Colleges and Schools: http://www.sacscoc.org/
- WASC Senior College and University Commission: http://www.wascweb.org/

The regional accrediting organizations review schools in their entirety. Both public and private and two- and four-year schools can be reviewed. Holding regional accreditation should allow credits to transfer smoothly between different member schools depending upon the established transfer criteria at the receiving institution. Remember: Ultimately, the college or university you are trying to transfer into has final say on credit transferability.

Nontraditional education usually requires national accreditation but not necessarily. Nontraditional education is vocational training through a vocational school or career-technical school that leads to a completed apprenticeship or certification. Vocational education is a means of training future workers with skills more directly relevant to the evolving needs of the workforce. Vocational education encompasses such fields as electrician, welding, and phlebotomy. Did I catch you? Are you wondering what that word means? Phlebotomists are the individuals who draw your blood at the hospital. Phlebotomy is a common pathway for many hospital corpsmen. These types of career fields are more hands-on and technical in nature.

Many nationally accredited schools can offer students successful pathways to promising careers. The programs are designed to get students into the workforce as soon as possible and can usually be completed in two years or less, significantly faster than a four-year bachelor's degree.

According to the president of the Council for Higher Education Accreditation (CHEA), out of the four main accrediting agencies, two award national accreditation—both national faith-related and national career-related. The national faith-related accreditors work with institutions that have religious affiliations and are mostly nonprofit, degree-awarding institutions. The national career-related accreditors work with mostly for-profit, degree- and non-degree-awarding institutions. [4]

To search for a specific school's accreditation or a particular program of interest, go online (at http://www.chea.org/search/default.asp) and agree to the search terms. You can also complete a search of the national accrediting agencies that the U.S. Department of Education considers reliable (go to http://ope.ed.gov/accreditation/).

You do not necessarily need to attend a nationally accredited college for vocational education. Credits from nationally accredited schools will not transfer into regionally accredited schools. This can cause significant issues down the road if a student ever decides to pursue more credits in higher education. Many state community and technical colleges offer vocational training programs that award associate degrees or certificates. There are positives to attending a community college as well. For example, if you complete a certificate program in welding at a state community college that also offers an associate degree in welding, you should be able to transfer those credits toward the associate at a later date if you decide to pursue higher education.

Last of all, and not to confuse you even more, programmatic accreditation is needed for certain degrees above and beyond the institutional accreditation. Programmatic accreditation organizations focus on specific courses of study offered at a college or university. Degree pathways such as law, engineering, and nursing require that the course of study receive special accreditation, and the institutional accreditation of the school is not sufficient. Attending a program that maintains programmatic accreditation can help your degree be more effective (as in getting you a job!) or make earned credit hours more transferable.

If you are not sure whether your degree requires programmatic accreditation, search CHEA's website (http://www.chea.org/Directories/special.asp) for further information.

To search for a particular institution's accreditation, use the following websites:

http://www.ope.ed.gov/accreditation/
http://www.chea.org/search/default.asp
http://nces.ed.gov/collegenavigator/

ADMISSIONS REQUIREMENTS

Every institution will have its own set of admissions requirements. Some, like community colleges and many vocational schools, maintain open admissions. Others, mainly four-year institutions of higher learning (universities), have a predetermined set of admissions qualifications that can be quite rigorous. Many institutions are starting to offer flexible admissions to veterans. This section will discuss the possible requirements for admissions into colleges and vocational schools.

State-Based Community and Technical Schools

Entrance into the local community or technical college is typically much less stressful than entrance into four-year universities. Attending community college is a great way to get started with school for Marines who have little or no time to prepare the required documents or manage application deadlines. Many Marines return from deployment and separate from the military in less than a month. With deadlines for university admissions passing as early as ten months prior to class start dates, community college is sometimes the only option available.

State-based community and technical colleges may offer or require the following:

- Open admissions
- In most cases, students can be accepted with or without a high school diploma or GED
- Possible early-bird registration for active-duty military and veterans
- May require an application fee
- Registration deadlines
- Many specific, high-demand programs may be impacted (too many applicants and not enough available open spots), require special entrance criteria (prerequisite classes), and have a waitlist for start times
- English and math placement tests are typically taken to determine proper level placement
- Admissions application is typically online and only takes a few minutes
- Supporting documents may be necessary—for example, high school transcripts, military transcripts, and residency proof
- Proof of immunizations

Four-Year Colleges and Universities

Four-year institutions of higher learning usually have selective admissions with application requirements and deadlines. Some may offer veterans flexible admissions, but in most cases veterans will follow the same pathway as civilians. A written timetable of deadlines for all materials can be obtained by contacting the school and checking the admissions sections of the website. Be prepared to put in a fair amount of time preparing.

College and university admissions may require the following:

- An application (in most cases, this can be done online)
- Application fees
- ACT and SAT test scores (see the "SAT and ACT" section of chapter 8)
- Essays
- Letters of recommendation
- Student must have followed a college pathway in high school meeting minimum subject requirements
- High school and college transcripts
- Minimum high school GPA
- Minimum high school class rank
- Demonstration of community service (military service may fulfill this requirement)
- Proof of immunizations

Vocational-Technical and Career Colleges

Depending upon the program a student is applying to within the school, admission requirements may vary. In certain fields, such as nursing, entrance exams may be mandatory. Exams can include physical fitness tests, basic skills exams, and Health Education Systems, Inc. (HESI), entrance exams.

Always do careful research into the career you are choosing to determine if your certification or license from a career college is valid. States often have mandatory requirements pertaining to the fields of education taught at a technical school, and students need to verify that the school meets these standards. Always check on the state government website. Many state websites list the state-approved programs right on the site.

Typically, admissions are open with a few minimum requirements, such as the following:

- High school transcript and diploma or GED
- Completed admissions forms
- An interview
- Statement of general health
- Any mandatory subject-specific exams

Leadership Scholar Program

The Leadership Scholar Program (LSP) may give qualified applicants an admissions advantage. The program is not designed to help students bypass admissions requirements, but it may help streamline the acceptance process. If a transitioning Marine (this program is not available to service members in other branches) meets the program requirements and the college or university requirements, he or she might be eligible to hook onto LSP.

LSP assists active-duty and reserve, honorably discharging Marines in gaining acceptance into colleges and universities throughout the United States. The Marine Corps partnered with over two hundred institutions of higher learning in order to facilitate a smoother transition for separating veterans who want to pursue a bachelor's degree. The free program aims to identify Marines who qualify for acceptance to school and helps them fast track their acceptance.

The purpose of the LSP is for schools to get Marines out of the mainstream selection process and to give qualified undergraduate applicants special consideration for acceptance. The program does not award any money to be used toward education. According to the individual currently running LSP, "an LSP recommendation adds significant weight to the application" and "essentially provides an advanced, singled out 'look' prior to the school admissions offices making final decisions."[5]

To qualify for LSP, a veteran must meet the following qualifications:

- Be honorably discharged, or be honorably discharged prior to the start of the first semester
- Be a high school graduate
- Have an Armed Forces Qualification Test (AFQT) score of 70 or above*
- Have a General Technical (GT) score of 115 or above*
- Be considered a college freshman or a transfer student
- Receive command endorsement

* If your scores are not sufficient, waivers may sometimes be granted, or you may be able to retest if you are still on active duty. The base education centers can offer further guidance on Armed Services Vocational Aptitude Battery (ASVAB) retesting policies.

Documents needed for submission to LSP:

1. One copy of all high school transcripts (unofficial)
2. One copy of all college transcripts (unofficial)
3. One copy of your Joint Services Transcript (JST; see https://jst.doded. mil)

4. Copies of NAVMC 118 (3) Chronological Record, (11) Administrative Remarks, *AND* (12) Offenses and Punishment; talk to adjutant/ IPAC (Installation Personnel Administration Center) if you need assistance with these records
5. Copies of your Record of Service (ROS), Basic Individual Record (BIR), Basic Training Record (BTR), awards page, and education record (TEDU) can be found on Marines Online (MOL)
6. Letter of recommendation (get as many as possible!)

The college entrance process can sometimes be confusing. LSP can help aid the admissions process and make it less painful. Several of the participating schools are Ivy League, such as Columbia, Harvard, and Yale. However, veterans do not have to be targeting an Ivy League school in order to jump on LSP. Many top state and private schools are also participating, such as the University of New Mexico and California State University, Fullerton. The website has a school-search-by-state section where veterans can look up participating schools and their acceptance requirements.

While each school sets its own entrance requirements, most institutions will want the following:

- High school transcripts
- College transcripts (for transfer students)
- JST transcripts and letters of recommendation
- Copies of NAVMC 118 (3), (11), *AND* (12); and copies of ROS, BIR, BTR, awards page, and education record

To search for a specific school's admissions requirements under LSP, click on the state the school is located within, and then click on the school's name. Each link lists the requirements and deadlines for students coming in under LSP, and some also offer helpful school-related information for veterans.

While LSP is designed for undergraduate students, the director has been extremely helpful in facilitating relationships between Marines who are searching out graduate programs and their institutions of choice.

MILITARY AWARENESS

Servicemembers Opportunity Colleges (SOC)

SOC was created to assist active-duty service members and their spouses in their pursuit of education. SOC operates in collaboration with higher education associations, the Department of Defense (DOD), and active and reserve components of the military. The Defense Activity for Non-Traditional Education Support (DANTES) manages the contract that is funded through the DOD. The group aims to improve higher education opportunities for active-duty military.

Service members often face numerous roadblocks when pursuing higher education during their active-duty time. The SOC Consortium tries to eliminate many of these roadblocks by working with educational institutions and creating higher degrees of flexibility. The point is to facilitate military degree completion as opposed to simply compiling course credits. The program is available to family members as well.

Attending SOC schools can benefit active-duty service members and veterans. SOC schools will take a look at a service member's JST (https://jst. doded.mil), formerly known as the SMART (Sailor Marine American Council on Education Transcript), and possibly award prior learning credit based on experience. More information on the JST can be found in the "Prior Learning Credit" chapter (chapter 7). For those who already read that chapter, you know that means the possibility of earning free college credit!

Not every school participates in the SOC Consortium. Currently, around 1,900 schools are enrolled with available associate, bachelors, and graduate-level programs. Consortium members offer their students reasonable transfer credit, reduced academic residency, credit for training (JST), and credit for testing programs such as the College-Level Examination Program (CLEP) or DSST (formerly "DANTES Subject Standardized Tests"). Find more information regarding these topics by visiting the SOC Consortium website (http://www.soc.aascu.org).

Service members already enrolled in a school can search for the school's status on the website. For example, if Corporal Jones were enrolled in Thomas Edison State College in New Jersey (online, of course!) for an associate degree and wanted to find more information about its affiliation with SOC, Corporal Jones should start on the SOC website.

Corporal Jones clicks on the "SOC Consortium" tab on the main website page and then clicks a search by either state or school name. Upon finding

"Thomas Edison," he clicks the tab and is taken to the school's website. Sometimes the link will take users directly to the SOC information page for the school. Other times, the link will go directly to the school's main page, and a search will need to be conducted to find the desired information.

In the case of Thomas Edison, Corporal Jones needed to search. He found the military/veterans tab clearly labeled on the main page, scrolled down to military degree completion, and found all kinds of information on SOC and the school. Many helpful resource links were also listed along the right-hand side of the page, and the program benefits were clearly outlined. Plus, the school did a great job of adding extra resource information that he might find useful. Lastly, Corporal Jones noted that the school has contact pathways strictly for veterans and active-duty military. This enables Marines to stream-line the academic process by eliminating anyone who does not understand their active-duty or veteran needs.

Many SOC schools also maintain MOS-related degrees. MOS-related de-grees enable Marines to maximize their military experiences and use them to facilitate college degrees. These degrees consist of pre-negotiated credit aligned with specific MOSs. Choosing a school with an MOS-related degree that you qualify for might enable you to save time and money. Remember that it limits the subject area you will study.

The SOC website has numerous search options. Students can search for schools, review the "Frequently Asked Questions" sections, and read *The Military Educator*, which is the newsletter of the Commission on Military Education and Training (CMET) and is distributed by SOC. The newsletter provides information on programs and services pertaining to the DOD Vol-untary Education Program. And you can find an article that I wrote in the April 2011 issue (at http://www.soc.aascu.org/pubfiles/socmisc/miled0411.pdf)!

SOCMAR Agreement

SOCMAR stands for the Servicemembers Opportunity Colleges Marine Corps Agreement. This is juicy information, so pay attention! SOCMAR schools are selected by the Corps to offer associate and bachelor's degrees to Marines and their dependents. If your school awards the SOCMAR, you definitely want to request one. You should have the agreement completed by the end of your first six credits.

The SOCMAR agreement has two major benefits:

1. It protects your degree plan.
2. It (potentially) locks in JST credits.

Let's talk about the SOCMAR and how it can lock in your degree plan. Gunnery Sergeant Bailey attended XYZ Community College, which was a SOCMAR-awarding institution. He went to the JST website and requested that his official transcript be sent to his school, declared for an associate degree in business, and received an official degree plan. Upon completion of six or more credits, he requested and received a SOCMAR.

Fast-forward to the end of his degree. He had three classes left to finish; the school contacted him regarding notification of a change to the business degree plan, and told him that he now had six classes to complete before the school would consider him for graduation. He was not happy, but he was able to produce a copy of his SOCMAR agreement, and the school was required to honor that initial agreement. This meant that he could not be forced to participate in classes he was not prepared to take. The SOCMAR locked the gunny and the school into the initial degree plan that both had agreed upon through the SOCMAR.

I want to point out that this is not a common occurrence. Schools do periodically change degree plans but not typically so often that you need to worry yourself at night.

The SOCMAR may also help you lock in any free JST credits your school awarded you, in case you need to transfer. This pathway can get sticky. Like I state in the JST chapter (chapter 7), credit awarded at one school may not be honored at another. Just as transferring regular academic credit is done at the discretion of the school you are trying to transfer into, so are JST credits.

The possibility exists that you could receive free JST elective credits from your school, try to transfer, and lose them all. For example, Staff Sergeant Ramirez attended ABC Community College, and the school awarded him twenty-one JST elective credits. He locked in a SOCMAR, finished the associate degree while on active duty, and then, after separation, tried to transfer to a four-year university that did not participate in the SOCMAR agreement. The university informed him that they would not honor the twenty-one JST credits he was awarded through ABC College. He was aware beforehand that this might happen and he could potentially have to make up those credits. He was not upset, since he knew what he was getting into prior to making the decision. He still had the associate degree and was able to list it on his résumé. If you remain aware of the possibility that in a transfer situation you might have to play catch-up, you will be a well-informed student and better able to prepare in case this does occur.

Many Marines get upset when they hear this sad news. Remember that the awarding of JST credit is ultimately up to the schools; therefore, each particular school holds the determining power. Now, if you transfer from one SOCMAR-awarding school to another SOCMAR-awarding school, you will be guaranteed a smooth transfer of all credit, including any freebie JST you were awarded. When schools agree to award the SOCMAR, they agree to the guaranteed transfer process.

This pathway is easy to facilitate for Marines who remain on active duty. For example, every school aboard Camp Pendleton is SOCMAR awarding. Transferring from one of the community colleges into one of the universities is an easy process, and very often Marines pursue this pathway and fast track their degrees. Trouble begins when Marines try to transfer college credit without completing a bachelor's degree. Others do not finish the associate while on active duty, but hope to transfer all traditional credit and JST credit without trouble upon separation. Unfortunately, this is not always easy, and Marines will most likely have makeup work to complete.

The SOCMAR-awarding associate and bachelor's degree institution list is not enormous, but it is rapidly growing. Check the list (at http://www.soc.aascu.org/socmar/Default.html). Even if your school is not on the list, you should contact the institution to enquire if they will evaluate your JST for potential prior learning credit.

Chapter Five

Admissions Process

Most schools generally follow the same admissions process, even though the requirements can change drastically from school to school. No matter if a student is an incoming freshman, a transfer student, or a potential vocational student, the pathway to gain admittance will follow the same route, but it may vary in difficulty. Prospective students at schools with an open enrollment policy will normally have a less intensive pathway to admittance. Students pursuing schools with selective admissions will spend more time preparing.

A typical pathway follows a route like this:

1. Pick a school or schools, call the veterans' representatives, discuss admissions requirements, and decide on an institution.
2. Apply (usually online).
3. Receive acceptance.
4. Apply for Tuition Assistance (TA), the GI Bill, or Federal Student Aid (FSA).
5. Register for classes (choose classes based on a degree plan).

PICK A SCHOOL

Contacting the veterans' representatives should initially give you a good feel of a school's perspective toward its veteran students. The vet reps have been there, done that already. If there are any tricks to gaining admission, they will know. Also, it enables you to identify yourself as a veteran, active-duty service member, or military spouse. The admission's pathway, cost, and required documents may be different from those for the civilian population, and the vet reps will be able to guide you in your quest for the appropriate resources.

Request that you receive pertinent information in some manner, whether paper-based or online resources. You will need to know all relevant information, including application deadlines, registration deadlines, financial aid timelines, class start dates, dorm-based information (if applicable) or in-town housing options, and who your point of contact will be for GI Bill concerns and for your Certificate of Eligibility. This topic is covered in depth in the "Cost and Payment Resources" chapter (chapter 6).

Contacting the veterans' department of your school of choice should be a top priority. If you find it difficult to get in touch with the representatives at your chosen location, that is not a good sign. The veterans' department at the school is your support system. If you cannot find anyone prior to attending the institution, how easy will they be to find when you are in residence?

APPLY

You have finished your research and settled on a particular school or schools. Now it is time to apply. Make sure you verify with the vet reps if you need to pay the application fee. I have found many schools that waive the fee for active-duty military and veterans.

Check the school's website prior to applying. In most cases, schools list an application checklist on their admissions page. This should help you prepare all relevant documents, such as your Joint Services Transcript (JST), DD-214, personal statement, SAT scores, or immunization records, in advance.

Oftentimes the application checklist for a four-year college or university does not list a personal statement, but when you begin the process it will surprise you partway through. Personal statement length requirements can be in the range of 350–3,000 words.

Writing a personal statement should not be nerve-racking, although many Marines feel tremendous stress during this experience. Most of the stress is just about finding a starting point. Once you get going, you will find the experience to be a good precursor to your new college life; after all, college does require a fair amount of writing. Here are a few steps to guide you through your personal essay.

Step 1

If you are having trouble starting, try brainstorming. I recommend sticking to topics around your military experience. Usually, I can find lots of good topics from just asking a Marine about his or her time in the service. Here are some of the questions I ask:

1. Why did you join the military?
2. What do you do in the military?
3. Does it require specialized training? What kind?
4. Did you go anywhere interesting to conduct that training? (Okinawa? Djibouti?)
5. Have you deployed? Where to? What did you do while deployed?
6. Did you experience combat? How did it make you feel?
7. Did you work with service members from other countries on your deployment? What were the cultural differences?
8. Did your deployments or combat experiences help shape the decisions you are making now? Is that why you are pursuing higher education?

Step 2

After this, you can typically pick a subject and narrow down the talking points. Sometimes it helps to brainstorm topics that interest you on paper and see if there are overlapping subjects. Many Marines feel that they do not do anything exciting in the military. That is definitely not true. Everything Marines do is exciting to civilians. My daily drives on base prove that fact to me. I see Marines practicing martial arts, simulating combat casualty assistance, and operating convoys heavily laden with weapons. Where else can you see these types of activities? Maybe it is all in a day's work for a Marine, but civilians find it fascinating.

Step 3

Once you settle on a topic, write it down on a piece of paper. Think about the topic, and write brief statements about everything that comes to your mind surrounding it. For example:

I joined the military after I graduated high school because I come from a military family.

- Work
- Timing
- Patriotism
- Security
- The war

Once you have a list drawn up, you need to add more layers to discuss. Here is an example:

- Work: productive suffering, meaningful work equals personal satisfaction, physical work, community environment
- Timing: graduated high school or college, came of age, rite of passage
- Patriotism: American flags, pledge of allegiance, 9/11 firefighters, serve my country, family military history, higher calling
- Security: airports, military bases, national events, worldwide, job security, pay, career
- The war: participate, serve my country, combat veteran, benefits, test of strength and willpower, face the unknown, perseverance

Step 4

Think about the notes you have written. Narrow down your subject or topic by eliminating areas that don't seem to fit. For example, I think the section on security does not follow the theme of the other topics. When I review each section, it seems that I joined the military after high school graduation because it is a rite of passage that occurs in my family. The military taught me good work values and community involvement. I was able to participate in the war, which bolstered my perseverance to succeed. Somehow the security section does not seem to fit with the rest, so I am eliminating it.

Step 5

Organize your thoughts in a good writing order, and start thinking about expanding the topics into a paper format.

- Patriotism: American flags, pledge of allegiance, 9/11 firefighters, serve my country, family military history, higher calling
- Timing: graduated high school or college, came of age, rite of passage
- Work: productive suffering, meaningful work equals personal satisfaction, physical work, community environment for the greater good
- The war: participate, serve my country, combat veteran, benefits, test of strength and willpower, face the unknown, perseverance

Now you need to determine why this experience shaped your current perspectives on education and organize the above-listed thoughts into a logical written order. You should also start thinking about your career goals, your character strengths, and why you have chosen this particular institution. Below, I have labeled each group in the order I feel it belongs to write an effective personal statement.

- Patriotism: American flags, pledge of allegiance, 9/11 firefighters, serve my country, family military history, higher calling (2)
- Timing: graduated high school or college, came of age, rite of passage (1)
- Work: productive suffering, meaningful work equals personal satisfaction, physical work, community environment for the greater good (3)
- The war: participate, serve my country, combat veteran, benefits, test of strength and willpower, face the unknown, perseverance (4)

Before you begin writing your essay, you need to consider your audience. Here are a few questions to consider while writing:

- Who is going to read this essay?
- What does the reader already know about this subject, and why is it important?
- What do I want the reader to know about this subject?
- What part of my topic is the most interesting?

Your reader could be a dean at the school, an academic counselor, a professor, or the like. Most likely, this individual has no knowledge of your topic if you write about a particular military experience, but do not discount the fact that he or she could also be a veteran. You need to explain why this experience shaped your decisions moving forward. You want them to see you in a different light compared to other applicants. You want your essay to stand apart and be more memorable than all of the others. Make sure to pick a topic that you can easily write about and that will attract interest.

Here is a sample essay written based upon the above process:

> After graduating high school in June of 2004, I enlisted in the United States Marine Corps. I come from a long line of Marine Corps infantryman, and I wanted to follow in the family tradition. Both Iraq and Afghanistan were combat-laden hotspots at this time. My family was worried, but after watching the September 11, 2001, terrorist attacks on television during my freshman year, I knew I could not Pledge Allegiance to the Flag every morning without following the call I felt to serve.
>
> Not long after completing my training, I found myself patrolling the streets of Ramadi, Iraq, coming under constant fire. The Marine Corps trained me how to respond during high-stress situations, and these experiences taught me the value of community involvement. Our cooperative teamwork saved us on numerous occasions. The preparation and training we went through as a group prior to deploying paid off when we needed it most. Iraq was a meaningful experience for me. It shaped my perspective on hard work and productive suffering.
>
> Although I love the Corps, getting shot at repetitively changed my outlook on life. I am ready for the next chapter, my education. Compared to most, I know what it takes to succeed. I have learned that skill in the Marine Corps. I know that success takes teamwork and willpower.
>
> I chose to attend XYZ University because of their reputation as leaders in the field of community involvement. The university offers a holistic approach to the education of its students, and I feel my background will be respected and put to use to enhance the effort and learning of my peers. The university's Veterans' Center offers numerous services to assist me should I need anything and offers many opportunities for veteran interaction.
>
> I hope that XYZ University will take the time to consider me as a prospective freshman student. If selected for admission, I will enhance the professor's learning environments, and I know that working together we can make the classroom more productive and challenging.

Make sure to create your JST account (see the "Prior Learning Credit" chapter, chapter 7), and be prepared to send your official transcripts to the school immediately. While many schools will take these at a later date, the earlier you submit them, the faster your application process can be completed.

You will also need to apply for your FSA (see chapter 6 on cost and payment resources) at this time. If you are applying to multiple schools, you can list up to ten on the federal aid application. This might lead to free federal money for educational expenses that does not need to be paid back!

RECEIVE ACCEPTANCE

For most open enrollment schools, official acceptance is given quickly. For schools with selective admissions, official acceptance is often sent out many months later. Check the school's website for reporting dates, or ask the vet reps. I have found a few schools with selective admissions able to give almost immediate acceptance or denial to veterans—for example, DePaul University in Chicago and Robert Morris University in Pennsylvania.

In most cases, your acceptance letter or your student account website will tell you the next steps you must make. These steps may include payment of fees to hold your spot in the school or for on-campus housing. This is typical for face-to-face schooling. Most active-duty service members pursuing school will not have these extra fees. Determine the final date for reimbursement of these fees in case you decide to attend another school at the last minute. That way, you will not be stuck losing money!

APPLY FOR TUITION ASSISTANCE, GI BILL, OR FEDERAL STUDENT AID

You have received your school acceptance letters and decided upon an institution. Now it is time to activate your GI Bill or apply for TA to pay for your schooling. If you are still on active duty, you should contact the local education center and inquire about TA. You will need to attend a College 101 Brief (if you have not already done so). College 101 is mandatory for first-time TA users. You can read more pertaining to TA in chapter 6.

If you are already separated or soon will be, it is time to activate your GI Bill. If you rate both the Montgomery GI Bill (MGIB) and Post 9/11, chapter 6 will help you decipher which one to choose. The veterans' representatives at your school of choice should be able to help as well. The GI Bill section of chapter 6 will explain how to apply to get your benefit rolling.

If you have a state-based benefit that pertains to your situation, you may need a bit more one-on-one help to determine your best pathway. Review the explanation of the benefits available to you in chapter 6 carefully before committing to either federal GI Bill. In some states, veterans can bring in more money by double dipping on state-based educational benefits and MGIB, compared to those under strictly Post 9/11. Again, if you cannot decipher the best pathway on your own, contact the vet reps at your school for advice on what other veterans have decided upon. Never just take a guess about the benefits, since it could mean missing out on hundreds of dollars every month.

Now is also the time to apply for your FSA. Remember that TA and the GI Bills only go so far. TA does not cover books, computers, or tools, and it is capped at $250 per semester credit hour. FSA money can help bridge any leftover gaps.

REGISTER FOR CLASSES

You will need to meet with an academic counselor in order to choose the appropriate classes for your degree. If attending school online, oftentimes your academic counselor will email you a degree plan. The degree plan lists every required class you need to take to attain your declared degree or certification.

Typically, degree plans will also reflect any free military credits the school awards you based on the information provided in your JST. Most schools will not inform you of the evaluation outcome until the end of your second class, so more guidance may be needed from an academic counselor prior to class selection for the first term. Starting with general education subjects is a safe route. Most of the time military credits only knock out elective credits, and general education subjects in a traditional degree pathway are always necessary.

If you need help registering for classes, you may want to visit the registrar's office of your school. In most cases, face-to-face registration will still be possible. You may also need to check to determine if a "hold" has been placed on your account. Sometimes, for reasons such as the TA voucher not arriving on time or missing documents, your account may be on hold. The registrar can tell you why.

Always be aware of the registration deadlines. Check with your school to see if the institution offers early bird registration for active-duty service members or veterans. This is an especially crucial step for veterans using their GI Bills. The VA will cover only classes listed on your degree plan (just like TA). Early bird registration allows veterans to get their pick of classes over the civilian population. Basically, every class you want should be open. If you miss these deadlines, you may have trouble getting into the classes you need to maintain full-time status according to the VA (full-time status = full-time housing allowance on Post 9/11). Plus, if you miss the final deadline, you may lose your spot at the school.

Veterans will most likely need to produce a copy of their DD-214 to the veterans' department at the school to prove benefit eligibility. It is a good idea to always keep a copy on hand along with your student identification number. Active-duty service members may need a copy of their orders to be aboard the base where they are currently stationed. Oftentimes, the local community colleges will want to see a copy of these orders in order to grant the service member in-state tuition. Spouses may need a copy of the orders as well as their dependent identification card in order to be given the in-state tuition rate. Make sure your spouse has access to a copy of your orders just in case you deploy. Spouses using transferred Post 9/11 benefits should keep a copy of their service member's DD-214 if he or she has already separated.

If you previously attended another school, you will need to have those transcripts sent to the new institution for evaluation. In most cases, the transcripts will need to go from the old school directly to the new one in order to remain official. Having a couple spare sets of transcripts on hand is usually a smart idea. Once a transcript is opened, it is no longer considered official, so order an extra one for yourself. You should take a copy of the transcript with you to meet with your academic counselor to help guide your class selections prior to your official transcripts being evaluated. No point in taking a class you already took!

You are most likely ready to matriculate at this point. Marines always stare at me in confusion at this point, but never fear: matriculation is not difficult! At a community college, you will need to take the math and English placement tests and determine your starting point for these two classes. If you test below college freshman level, the school will put you in remedial classes. This is not a big deal, but it can slow down progress. These classes will help boost your baseline skill level and make you more successful in your future classes. If you would like to boost your math and English skills prior to taking the placement test, check out http://www.petersons.com/DOD and click on the "Online Academic Skills Course (OASC)" link. OASC is like an online self-paced Military Academic Skills Program (MASP) class. Matriculation usually requires an orientation session. Some schools offer the orientation in an online format; others require you to physically attend. Your academic counselor should inform you when your paperwork has been processed and you have an official degree plan on file. Then you have matriculated!

All of the initial hard work to start school is done at this point. Now you need to prepare for everything else. If you are a veteran, you may need housing. Check with the vet reps for recommendations. Many Marines find roommates through the vet reps, the Facebook page for veterans attending the school, or the student veterans' associations. I know a Marine who found a roommate when he called the vet reps at his school about a possible list, and the vet rep who answered the phone desperately needed a roommate himself and had previously been stationed aboard the same base. It was good luck and definitely eased the fears of the transitioning Marine.

Start checking out all of the veteran services offered aboard the school campus or in the surrounding areas. Knowing where the services are located may save you heartache and time later on. Some of the services offer outreach, and some of the services might be strictly for socialization or networking. Take advantage of both.

If you have served in a combat zone, find your closest VA Vet Center (at http://www.va.gov/directory/guide/vetcenter_flsh.asp). The Vet Centers can help eligible veterans with counseling, outreach, and referral services to help with postwar readjustment to civilian life. Research the VA service (go to http://www.vetcenter.va.gov/index.asp).

Student veteran organizations that are school specific operate aboard many campuses. Usually, you can find their information right on the school's website. The Student Veterans of America (http://www.studentveterans.org/) connects veterans through social media outlets to offer support and promote student vet success. Participating in an organization can help veterans integrate into their local veteran community. Veterans who seek out other veterans typically have higher success rates. Veterans who isolate themselves may find themselves having difficulty transitioning.

Chapter Six

Cost and Payment Resources

Cost is often a major factor for students when picking a college or vocational program to attend. Active-duty service members should try to attend institutions that fall within the parameters of Tuition Assistance (TA). Veterans should consider GI Bill coverage while researching potential schools. Why pay for school when you have coverage? If you can stay within these parameters, you might come out of your educational experience completely debt free.

The following topics will be covered within this section:

- Financial goals
- Marine Corps Tuition Assistance (TA)
- Montgomery GI Bill (MGIB) (http://www.gibill.va.gov)
- Post 9/11 (http://www.gibill.va.gov)
- VA GI Bill Feedback System
- GI Bill Application and Conversion Process
- Transfer of Post 9/11 to dependents
- Yellow Ribbon Program (http://www.gibill.va.gov)
- State-based veteran education benefits
- Federal Student Aid (http://www.fafsa.ed.gov)
- GI Bill Top-Up (http://www.gibill.va.gov)
- Scholarships (including dependents)
- Textbook-buying options

FINANCIAL GOALS

Transitioning from the military is a difficult process without also having to worry about finances. Veterans who prepare in advance will have less stress during the process and will be able to focus on their studies more effectively. Having minimal distractions during school will enable veterans to achieve a higher degree of academic success. Successfully educated or trained veterans will be more productive in their future endeavors and able to enrich their surrounding civilian communities.

Bypassing the work option, veterans have three main sources of income while attending school:

- GI Bill housing stipend
- Federal Student Aid (Pell Grant)
- Unemployment

If a veteran is able to maximize benefits under each of these three options, he or she will have a good starting base (and, ideally, will not have to worry about daily stressors, like making rent, gas, and food).

The housing stipend on the Post 9/11 GI Bill is not typically enough to take care of one individual's personal needs, especially since "break pay" money is not paid while the student is not physically in school. The "Post 9/11" section later in this chapter explains that the housing allowance is pro-rated, and veterans will most likely not be receiving as much money as they expect.

Federal Student Aid Pell Grant money can be a great benefit for veterans attending school. Think about having an extra $5,730 per academic year to help with education-related expenses above and beyond the GI Bill. How much better off would you be for spending thirty minutes to fill out the FAFSA? The time will be well spent, especially if you are awarded assistance.

Since your previous year's tax information is required to fill out the FAFSA, you need to pay attention upon your initial separation from active duty. If you have recently separated from the military, your tax information may not reflect your current financial situation. For example, if Sergeant Smith separated in July 2014 and began college in August 2014, he would need to submit his 2013 taxes, which reflect his sergeant pay, on the FAFSA. The main problem is that he is no longer working and receiving this level of pay. In most cases, a veteran's pay is drastically reduced upon separation. If

Sergeant Smith does not receive an award or does not receive the full amount, he needs to visit his financial aid counselor to have his listed income level readjusted. Hopefully, upon readjustment of his income, he will be eligible for the maximum amount of Pell Grant award. Be aware that Pell Grant money is based on your tax information, so it will fluctuate from person to person depending upon their household finances.

The Unemployment Compensation for Ex-Servicemembers (UCX) program may help eligible separating service members rate some level of unemployment. Unemployment will vary state by state because the Law of the State determines how much money an individual can receive, the length of time to remain eligible, and any other eligibility conditions. Veterans must have been honorably separated in order to be eligible. Information on unemployment can be found on the U.S. Department of Labor's website: http://workforcesecurity.doleta.gov/unemploy/uifactsheet.asp.

Contact your local State Workforce Agency (http://www.servicelocator.org/OWSLinks.asp) upon separation to determine eligibility and apply. Make sure to have a copy of your DD-214.

Some military members may also receive a service-connected disability percentage; others may not. When you separate from the military, you will be screened by the VA to determine if you sustained any injuries or diseases while on active duty, or if any previous health-related issues were made worse by active military service. If you receive a minimum rating of 10 percent or higher, you may be eligible to receive a tax-free stipend from the VA every month. Zero percent ratings do not have a monetary stipend attached; however, in the "State-Based Veteran Education Benefits" section of this chapter, you can also see that many states offer benefits that are tied in to these disability ratings. For example, in California a 0 percent rating equals free school at state-supported institutions for your children. If you receive a percentage rating, this may help with your expenses. Be aware that ratings can take as long as twelve months to be determined, and there is such a thing as no rating at all.

Make sure to get screened prior to exiting the military. If you are not sure where to go, find your local VA office; it might even be right aboard the base you are stationed. The Disabled American Veterans (DAV) and the Veterans of Foreign Wars (VFW) maintain offices aboard several Marine Corps Bases and may assist you as well. Many academic institutions have visiting representatives from these organizations. They will help you with your initial claim if you did not make it while still on active duty. They can also help you submit for a claims adjustment if your medical situation has changed.

MARINE CORPS TUITION ASSISTANCE (TA)

TA is a voluntary education program for active-duty military. The program is designed to help Marines afford and pursue higher education while they remain on active duty without digging into their GI Bills.

To qualify for TA as of fiscal year 2014 (FY14), Marines must meet the following prerequisites:

1. Attend a College 101 Brief aboard a Marine Corps Base.
2. Have a General Technical (GT) score of 100 or above.*
3. Enlisted Marines must have at least sixty days remaining on contract after the class end date.
4. Officers must agree to remain on active duty for two years after final class completion.
5. Reserve officers must have an end of active service (EAS) date of at least two years after the class end date.
6. First-time applicants must have been in the service for at least twenty-four months.
7. Must have completed the Personal Finance MCI (3420F).
8. Must be eligible for promotion per MCO P1400.32D CH2.
9. Receive command approval.

* If a Marine does not have the required GT score, he or she will need to sit for the Test of Adult Education (TABE). The TABE checks the test taker's skill level in five areas:

1. reading comprehension
2. language
3. spelling
4. math computation
5. applied math

TABE scores through 12.9, which signifies the end of the senior year in high school. Marines must score a minimum of a 10.2 or higher in order to be eligible for TA. A score of 10.2 signifies proficiency through the second month of the sophomore year of high school.

The Education Centers aboard the bases do not maintain study material for the TABE. The free http://www.petersons.com/DOD website has a link called "Online Academic Skills Course" (OASC), which offers math and English refreshers. Reviewing this information prior to taking the TABE might help test takers clean out the cobwebs before testing. TABE test preparation can also be found on the Internet for free. Give a few of the following links a try:

http://www.studyguidezone.com/pdfs/tabeteststudyguide.pdf
http://www.testprepreview.com/tabe_practice.htm
http://www.youtube.com/watch?v=Wam25OG3UnU

If the TABE test is not passed on the first try, the student may try again; however, the Education Centers typically refer Marines to the thirty-day TAD Military Academic Skills Program (MASP) at this point.

TA Parameters

1. Covers up to $250 per semester credit hour, $166 per quarter hour, and $16.67 per clock hour.
2. Awards a maximum of $4,500 per fiscal year (from October 1 to September 15).
3. Does not cover fees, books, computers, and so on.
4. TA must be paid back if attending a class at the undergraduate level and student receives a grade of "F," or if attending at the graduate level and a grade of "D" or below is received.
5. TA must be paid back if class is dropped voluntarily after the 100 percent drop/add date.
6. TA must be paid back if an incomplete course is reported.
7. Marines using TA can only pursue one educational goal at a time.
8. Courses are funded at registration and may not exceed twelve months in duration.
9. Students must maintain a minimum of a 2.0 GPA at all times.
10. Students can apply for TA no more than thirty days before the start date of their class.
11. Funds are disbursed in a first-come, first-served fashion.

Web-Based TA

TA for the Marine Corps is now web based. All of the above-mentioned requirements still apply. After a Marine meets these requirements, he or she can visit https://myeducation.netc.navy.mil/ and register for a new account. The site can be accessed through Common Access Card (CAC) or by user name and password. When registering as a new user, the site will automatically kick users over to Navy Knowledge Online (https://www.nko.navy. mil). Marines register for their user name and password, and then return to the My Education website in order to access it without a CAC card.

Marines must have specific codes entered by Education Center personnel in order to gain full access to the site. Oftentimes, this requires a counseling appointment. Once all personal information has been verified or input, Marines may follow along the pages to apply for TA for each class. An officer's usmc.mil email address will be required in order to have command approve the TA request prior to the local Education Center's review of the document. Marines need to verify with their commands which officer is currently conducting approval for TA.

Once a Marine has submitted his or her TA request, the officer listed will receive an email informing him or her of the request. The TA request simultaneously populates within the local Education Center's list. Once command approves the request, assigned individuals at the Education Center will review the document and the applicant to determine if everything is up to HQMC standards. If so, the document will be approved if funds are available; otherwise, the applicant will be contacted for further explanation.

Once the final approval has been given, the applicant will be able to print his or her approved TA voucher directly from the My Education website without having to physically go to the Education Center. During the entire process, applicants will receive program-generated emails notifying them of their progress through the process.

The Camp Pendleton MCCS Joint Education Center website (http://www. mccscp.com/jec) has a downloadable packet that walks TA applicants through the process step by step. It does not matter which base you are stationed at; the process will be the same.

Distant and deployed Marines will now have easier access to TA through the web TA application process. If you are currently deployed and need extra assistance, contact your base's Education Center for guidance. A good place to start is the MCCS website of your particular base. Typically, the education centers post relevant information and contact numbers on their webpage.

Prepare in advance for all funding possibilities by checking out a few other options. Federal Student Aid (FSA) money is a great source of funding if you are eligible. Marines are often awarded Pell Grant money from FSA, which is the financial aid money for school that does not need to be repaid. These students are often able to continue their educations throughout the year even if they reach their TA fiscal year funding caps.

College-Level Examination Program (CLEP) exams are another viable option that may increase your degree productivity without decreasing the money in your wallet. The first CLEP in each subject is free for active-duty military. CLEP has thirty-three exams in five areas, encompassing subjects typically covered in the first two years of college. Check "Federal Student Aid" in this chapter and the "Subject Matter Proficiency Exams" section of chapter 7 for more detailed information.

If you are interested in applying for TA, contact the local Education Center aboard your base for more assistance (you can also see Marine Corps Order 1560.25 and MARADMIN 456/13).

MONTGOMERY GI BILL (MGIB)

Not all service members have MGIB. When you entered the service, if you elected to opt in to MGIB and paid $100 per month for your first year of service to total $1,200, you might rate MGIB. You must be separated with an honorable discharge as well; that goes for most benefits. Double-check your eligibility on the GI Bill website (http://www.gibill.va.gov).

As of the 2014–2015 academic year, MGIB will pay $1,648 per month for up to thirty-six months for school. MGIB can be used for academic degrees, certificate programs, on-the-job training (OJT), correspondence classes, apprenticeship programs, and flight training. Benefits are good for ten years after separation from the military.

Some service members participated in the $600 Buy-Up Program under MGIB. For those who did, an extra $150 per month will be added to their MGIB payments. That amount per month pays you back your $600 investment in four months. Every month after that point, you are making money. If you cannot remember if you paid the optional Buy-Up Program, check with IPAC. For those who did not pay the money, check with the veterans' representatives at the school you are interested in attending before running off to pay it now. If you select Post 9/11, you forfeit the $600 that it takes to fully fund the Buy-Up. Smaller Buy-Up packages can be bought for pro-rated amounts. If you rate it and decide to stay under MGIB, you will most likely want to pay the Buy-Up for increased monthly payments. IPAC can make the Unit Diary entry prior to your EAS.

Currently, if you paid into MGIB, remain under MGIB, and exhaust all thirty-six months of the benefit, you may be able to extend out an extra twelve months on Post 9/11. Contact the VA for final eligibility determination on this pathway. This may enable you to save some benefit for a master's degree or a certificate program. The problem is that in most cases, MGIB will not cover all of your bills.

I have only found a few situations in which it makes more sense for the veteran to remain under MGIB instead of opting for Post 9/11. There are two big ones. The first is online-only schools, which I do not recommend because you might be missing out on the full housing stipend under Post 9/11. The second situation occurs when Marines attend school in a state with a full state-based benefit. The "State-Based Veteran Education Benefits" section of this chapter will review both of these circumstances and demonstrate why a veteran might elect to remain under MGIB. Prior to electing either GI Bill, it is best to discuss all available options. Contact your state VA to determine your available state benefits and learn how to use them. Contact the veterans' department at the institution you would like to attend and request guidance. Typically, the veterans' representatives can offer great advice pertaining to the best benefit pathway. They have already blazed the trail and learned the ropes for themselves. The VA also offers guidance and can be reached at 1-888-GIBILL-1.

POST 9/11

Post 9/11 is truly an amazing educational benefit available to veterans who rate it. To determine your eligibility, visit the website (http://www.gibill.va. gov). Basically, to rate 100 percent of Post 9/11, you need to meet these criteria:

- Served thirty-six consecutive months after September 11, 2001
- Received an honorable discharge

There are other categories for approval, but, like I have stressed at other points in this book, always check to determine your specific eligibility. In this case, contact the VA at 1-888-GIBILL-1.

The Post 9/11 GI Bill has three financial components built into the program: books and supplies, housing, and tuition.

Books and Supplies

Post 9/11 has a books and supplies stipend. The stipend is pro-rated at $41.67 per credit hour for a maximum of $1,000 per academic year. A regular full-time student, who requires a minimum of twelve credits per semester, would receive the full $1,000. Anything less than that gets pro-rated until the veteran goes below the 50 percent rate-of-pursuit mark. At that point, the GI Bill stops paying. The stipend is broken into two payments per academic year and lumped in with the first month of the housing stipend for each semester.

You should take note that $1,000 is not actually a great amount for books. Books can often run more than $200 per class. Many universities list the approximate costs of textbooks for the school year on their website. For example, California State University, Long Beach (CSULB), estimates their books at $1,788 for the 2013–2014 academic year. According to their calculations, $1,000 won't cut it for books. You definitely need to check into other options. The "Textbook-Buying Options" section in this chapter is dedicated to helping you find used or rental books.

Housing

The housing stipend gets slightly more complicated. Referred to as the Monthly Housing Allowance (MHA), it is equivalent to the salary for an E-5 with dependents and applies for everyone. That is great if you separated anywhere near E-5, but if you separated as a general, you will need to do some adjusting with your budget (sorry—that is my bad sense of humor!). DO NOT use an online calculator other than the one offered on http://www. gibill.va.gov, which is actually the U.S. Department of Defense calculator (direct link: https://www.defensetravel.dod.mil/site/bahCalc.cfm). This is the only valid website when it comes to determining your MHA based on the ZIP code of your school. That's right—the MHA is based on the ZIP code of your school, not your abode.

Tuition

Tuition under the Post 9/11 GI Bill can get complicated to explain. I am going to keep it simple. If you follow the most basic of parameters, you will not pay a dime for your school. Go outside of these parameters and you run into technical billing questions; in this case, you should contact the school you are interested in attending for further information.

If you are pursuing an undergraduate or graduate degree, plan on attending a state school in the state where you have residency, and finish your degree within the thirty-six months of benefit you have allotted, your schooling should be covered. The thirty-six months is enough for most bachelor's degrees if you stay on track because it equates to nine months of school per year over the course of four years. Traditionally, we do not usually attend school in the summer, although you may if you are interested. If one of these factors changes, so might your bill.

Veterans who chose to attend private school received $19,198.31 for the academic year 2013–2014 (www.gibill.va.gov/resources/benefits_resources/rates/CH33/Ch33rates080113.html). Anything above that amount and you run the risk of having to pay out of pocket. I state it this way because many schools participate in the Yellow Ribbon Program (http://www.gibill.va.gov/benefits/post_911_gibill/yellow_ribbon_program.html), and it may help to cover private school costs that come in above the maximum VA-allotted threshold or out-of-state tuition charges.

What about out-of-state tuition, you ask? Well, it is not covered under Post 9/11. However, you have chances of getting out-of-state tuition covered under Yellow Ribbon and possible state-based benefits. These topics will be covered later in this chapter.

As stated above, the VA will pay you the full-time housing allowance if you pursue school at the full-time rate. The VA considers twelve credit hours to be full-time. However, if you have no previous college credit and intend on pursuing a bachelor's degree, twelve credits per semester will not suffice. Most bachelor's degrees require students to complete 120 semester credit hours of specific subject matter in order to have the degree conferred on them. That equates to fifteen credit hours each semester, or five classes.

The college year runs similar to the high school year—two semesters each year over the course of four years. So, 120 semester hours breaks down to fifteen semester hours each semester to total thirty credits each year (freshman year: 30; sophomore year: 30; junior year: 30; senior year: 30—total: 120). If you follow the VA's minimum guidelines of twelve credits each semester, or four classes, you will run out of benefits at the end of your senior year but only have earned ninety-six semester credit hours, which are twenty-four credits shy of the 120 required. You will be out of benefits but will not have obtained your degree. The academic counselors at the school you attend will help you with your degree plans. If you need to make changes or have questions, contact them for further advice.

VA GI BILL FEEDBACK SYSTEM

http://www.benefits.va.gov/GIBILL/Feedback.asp

The VA has recently implemented a new system to handle complaints pertaining to issues involving the Principles of Excellence. Educational institutions that have agreed to abide by the specific guidelines of the program are agreeing to do the following:

- Inform students in writing (should be personalized) about all costs associated with education at that institution.
- Produce educational plans for military and veteran beneficiaries.
- Cease all misleading recruiting techniques.
- Accommodate those who are absent due to military requirements.
- Appoint a point of contact (POC) that offers education-related and financial advice.
- Confirm that all new programs are accredited before enrolling students.
- Align refund policies with Title IV policies (Federal Student Aid).

Schools that participate in the Principles of Excellence program can be found on the VA website (see http://www.benefits.va.gov/gibill/principles_of_ excellence.asp).

Complaints should be submitted when institutions participating in the program fall below the above-listed set of standards. Complaints are filed on subjects such as recruiting practices, education quality, accreditation issues, grade policies, failure to release transcripts, credit transfer, financial topics, student loan concerns, refund problems, job opportunities after degree completion, and degree plan changes and subsequent requirements. To file a complaint, visit the website and follow the directions.

GI BILL APPLICATION AND CONVERSION PROCESS

The application process for the GI Bill is not complicated; however, it does currently take approximately four to six weeks to receive the Certificate of Eligibility (COE) statement. Make sure to allot time for the wait prior to starting school. If you find yourself in a time crunch, check with your school to see if the institution might take a copy of the submitted application and let you get started.

If you have MGIB and you are positive you want to convert to Post 9/11, the process can be done at the same time you activate the benefit. While there is no need to do so prior to this point, some Marines are more comfortable making the switch while still on active duty.

To activate the GI Bill, you will need to access the Veterans Online Application (VONAPP; see http://vabenefits.vba.va.gov/vonapp/). You can also access it by going to the main GI Bill website (http://www.gibill.va. gov): select the "Post 9/11" link on the right-hand side, select "Get Started" on the left-hand side, select "Apply for Benefits," and lastly select "Apply Online." You will need three pieces of information before you proceed:

- Your school's name and address
- A bank account and routing number (VA is direct deposit)
- An address you will be at in the next four to eight weeks

The easiest way to prepare for the application process is to be accepted to your intended institution prior to applying to activate your benefit, but you can change the required information at a later date by contacting the VA at 1-888-GIBILL-1.

The VA does not send hard checks anymore. Inputting your bank account and routing numbers enables them to directly deposit your MHA and book stipend money. You may change this information at a later date if you change your bank.

The address you list will be where your COE is delivered. Marines living in the barracks might want to send their COEs to their parents' or another reliable family member's address. Just make sure that the individuals located at the listed address keep their eyes open for the document and inform you when it arrives. You will need to take that document to the veterans' representative at your school as soon as you receive it, because it is the school's ticket to receive payment from the VA. This is part of the process for you to receive the housing allowance.

Process of Applying

Upon entering the VONAPP website (http://vabenefits.vba.va.gov/vonapp/), you will be asked if you are a first-time VONAAP user; answer accordingly.

Next, you will be asked if you possess an eBenefits Account. I find this to be a difficult way to enter the site. If you respond that you do not have an eBenefits account, you will need to create a VONAPP account (this seems to be a much easier pathway!). Be aware that you will need an eBenefits account for all other VA-related concerns; however, applying directly through VONAPP will not disrupt that process. Once settled, select the "22-1990 Education Benefits" form to proceed. The VONAPP website will ask you information pertaining to your active-duty tours, prior education and training, upcoming start date for your school and training, pursuit of study (associate degree, bachelor's degree, graduate degree, or apprenticeship or on-the-job training), and so on.

If you are concerned about the questions on the 22-1990 or whether you are making the correct choices, contact the VA at 1-888-GIBILL-1. The veterans' representatives at your intended school are usually good sources of information as well. Check with your base's education center to see if they keep paper copies of the 22-1990s if you would like to see the required information in advance.

Once you receive the COE, you need to take it (that is, a copy!) to the veterans' representatives at your school. You will also need to send a copy of your DD-214 to your local VA processing center. When you finish filling out and submitting the 22-1990, the main page on the VONAPP will maintain two links (side by side) with required, printable information; one is your submitted application, and the other is your local processing center, which is oftentimes not in the same state. Some institutions will also want a copy of your DD-214 for verification purposes.

If you are transferring to a new school, you will need to fill out the 22-1995 form, but only if you are not changing GI Bill chapters. The 22-1995 form can be found on the VONAPP website.

POST 9/11 TRANSFERABILITY TO DEPENDENTS

Active-duty service members may be eligible to transfer their Post 9/11 GI Bill benefits to dependents. The transfer process requires a four-year commitment to stay in the military. If benefits are successfully transferred, certain rules apply while the service member remains on active duty.

To be eligible to transfer benefits, service members must be eligible for Post 9/11 and:

- have completed six years of active-duty service to transfer to a spouse;
- have completed ten years of active-duty service to transfer to a child;
- have four years remaining on contract (enlisted) or commit four more years (officer);
- *OR* is precluded by standard policy or statute from serving an additional four years (must agree to serve maximum time allowed by such policy).

Transfer must be approved the while service member is still in the Armed Forces.

In a nutshell, Marines need to have completed the required time in service, depending upon transferring to a spouse or a child, and have four years left on contract. The best time to complete the process is at the same time as a re-enlistment or extension package that gives the individual the required amount of payback time.

To transfer benefits, follow these steps:

- Verify your time in service.
- Visit the website (at http://www.benefits.va.gov/gibill/post911_gibill.asp).
- Click on the "Transfer of Entitlement" option.
- Follow the directions ("Apply Now").
- You will find yourself on the MilConnect webpage and will need to enter your CAC card or Defense Finance and Accounting Services (DFAS) account information.
- Click on the "Go to Transfer of Eligible Benefits" link on the right-hand side.
- Apply the needed information and submit—but you are not finished.
- Obtain a Statement of Understanding (SOU) from the website or the local Education Center aboard your base.
- Fill out all required information and take it to the appropriate individuals: Career Planners if you are enlisted, and WO Admin for officers.
- Career Planners will verify time in service.
- The Battalion Commanding Officer signs off on a Marine's application, and then the document must be routed through IPAC.
- Once transfer is approved, eligibility documents will be found in the Transfer Education Benefits (TEB) website (https://www.dmdc.osd.mil/milconnect/help/topics/transfer_of_education_benefits_teb.htm) for each individual, and the required time commitment that is necessary to complete the process will reflect in MOL.

Service members may revoke transferred benefits at any given time. Designated months may also be changed or eliminated though the website while on active duty or through a written request to the VA once separated.

Dependents who have received transferred benefits will need to apply to use the benefits through the VONAPP website (http://www.gibill.va.gov) in the "Post 9/11, Apply for Benefits" section. Dependents may also print the form (22-1990e) and send it into their nearest VA regional office. The form may be found online (at http://www.vba.va.gov/pubs/forms/VBA-22-1990e-ARE.pdf) and regional offices may also be found online (at http://www.benefits.va.gov/benefits/offices.asp).

Eligible dependents:

- spouse
- service member's children
- combination of spouse and children

Dependents must be in the Defense Enrollment Eligibility Reporting System (DEERS).

Spouses:

- May use the benefit immediately
- Are not entitled to the MHA while the service member remains on active duty but are entitled once the service member separates
- Are entitled to the book stipend
- May use the benefit for up to fifteen years from the service member's EAS date, just like the service member

Children:

- May use the benefit only after the service member has attained ten years on active duty
- May use the benefit while the parent is on active duty or after separation
- Must have obtained a high school diploma or equivalency certificate, or have turned eighteen
- May receive the MHA while a parent remains on active-duty status
- Are entitled to the book stipend
- Do not fall under the fifteen-year delimiting date; however, benefits must be used prior to turning twenty-six years old.

Marines can commit the required payback time of four years after separating from active duty and dropping into the reserves.

The current website and emails:

http://www.gibill.va.gov/benefits/post_911_gibill/transfer_of_benefits.
   html

Marine Corps Active Duty—Officers: tasha.lowe@usmc.mil

Marine Corps Active Duty—Enlisted: michael.a.peck@usmc.mil

Marine Corps Reserve: smb_manpower.cmt@usmc.mil

YELLOW RIBBON PROGRAM (YRP)

YRP is designed to serve two purposes:

- Help cover out-of-state tuition prior to the veteran gaining in-state tuition.
- Cover tuition above and beyond the maximum allowable rate for private school.

YRP is not automatic, and there are many stipulations to watch out for prior to determining if the benefit will work for your particular purpose. YRP does not pay the student any money.

Eligibility

- Must rate 100 percent of the Post 9/11 GI Bill
- Active-duty members of the military are not eligible, nor are their spouses; however, children of active-duty service members may qualify (if the active-duty parent is eligible for 100 percent of Post 9/11)

YRP potentially enables veterans to cover costs above and beyond the Post 9/11 GI Bill parameters. Not all schools participate, and a school's participation for one year does not guarantee participation in subsequent years. You do not need to maintain full-time status in order to be eligible for YRP. Summer terms may be eligible as well, but check with your particular institution.

Schools must re-establish their YRP program with the VA every year. This means, and I have seen it happen, that a school may participate one year but not the next. You could get left hanging. For example, a Marine corporal attended a well-known private school in Georgia. The school participated during her first year, but not the following years. She was out of pocket roughly $22,000 per year for her school at that point—ouch!

Schools may participate on different levels by limiting the amount of YRP spots available and the amount of money they offer. This can restrict veterans from considering certain institutions based on financial constraints. The following is a hypothetical breakdown:

- School A participates in YRP with unlimited spots and unlimited money. Therefore, you shouldn't pay out of pocket. But you still run the risk of the school choosing not to participate in upcoming years.
- School B participates with twenty spots and $4,000 per student. Therefore, you may or may not get one of those twenty spots (remember that it is first come, first serve!), and the VA will match the $4,000, effectively giving you an extra $8,000 toward tuition (this is a rough explanation of how it actually works).

You must also check to see how the program at your school is participating. Consider the following hypothetical situation:

- School C: This graduate-level business program participates with seventeen spots and $11,000 per student.
- School D: This graduate-level education program participates with four spots and $6,000 per student.

Notice that different programs within the same school may participate with different amounts of money and available spots.

Finally, a school may participate differently at the graduate level than it does at the undergraduate level. See the following example:

- School E participates at the undergraduate level with five spots and $8,000 per student.
- School F participates at the graduate level with three spots and $1,000 per student.

While it can become complicated to determine the benefit you may be eligible for, the vet reps at the school can usually offer sound advice. You can search YRP participating schools by state (at http://www.gibill.va.gov/gi_bill_info/ch33/yrp/yrp_list_2013.htm). However, I always recommend contacting the VA directly for solid confirmation that the school you are applying for does participate and to what degree.

Do not make the mistake of thinking that a small, off-the-beaten-path school might not fill its YRP seats. I spoke with a small community college in Washington State that participates in the YRP, wondering if they often fill their openings. At that time, Washington State did not have a state-based law that gave in-state tuition to out-of-state veterans, but it has since passed legislation so that veterans who meet the qualifications should receive the in-state tuition rate. Prior to speaking to the veterans' representative, I thought to myself that it was nice they had allotted so many spots even though they probably did not need them. I mean, how many out-of-state veterans were relocating to this rural area and needed help with out-of-state tuition? I was so wrong! The school had a waiting list for its YRP spots that was in the double digits. Apparently, while the school was located in a rural area, it was also the closest school to one of the state's main snowboarding mountains and maintained a fairly large veteran population. On the flip side, I was happy to hear that our veterans were getting some much-needed R&R after their military service, along with a good education.

If you intend on transferring, you must speak with your new school regarding YRP eligibility at their institution. Eligibility at one does not guarantee eligibility at another. If you take a hiatus from your school and were enrolled in YRP, you may get dropped for subsequent semesters. Before you make any decisions, talk with your academic advisor and/or veteran department. The more informed you are, the better you can plan.

STATE-BASED VETERAN EDUCATION BENEFITS

Aside from the federal GI Bills available for honorably discharged veterans, many states also have state-based benefits to help with education. Some of the benefits work quite liberally; others have stricter guidelines. At many institutions, it is possible to double-dip off MGIB and a state-based benefit to maximize monetary intake. This can potentially mean more money in the student's pocket or longer-lasting education benefits.

It is extremely important to figure out if you rate a state-based benefit and how that benefit works before you sign up for your federal GI Bill. In some cases, you can bring in more money monthly by staying under MGIB instead of opting for Post 9/11. If you opt for Post 9/11 and activate your GI Bill, then find out later you could have made more money under MGIB, it is too late. Once the Post 9/11 GI Bill is selected and activated, there is no going back.

In order to determine what benefits your state has to offer (or does not have to offer!), and if you are eligible, check with your state's Department of Veterans' Affairs Office (http://www.va.gov/statedva.htm). Oftentimes, the school's veterans' representatives have information on their particular state's education benefits, but always check with the state VA to verify all potential available benefits, including possibilities other than education.

I list and describe many of the state-based benefits later in this chapter. Remember that states may cancel, change, or add benefits throughout time. While I strive to be as accurate as possible, this book was compiled and written in 2014, and things change. Since you are the veteran, you need to double-check what you have available at any specific time.

I have found two situations where MGIB might be a better choice than Post 9/11, and I explain them below. Remember that you can always visit with an education counselor aboard your base for further advice, and a quick phone call to the veterans' representatives at the school can usually tell you which GI Bill veterans are opting for in the same situation.

Two examples that I have encountered with veterans who sometimes prefer to remain under MGIB are veterans who come from a state that has a full state-based education benefit, and in a few rare cases veterans who choose to attend school fully online. I do not recommend fully online school, because it usually means missing out on a good chunk of housing stipend money.

Here is an example of a veteran who did better by staying under MGIB instead of electing Post 9/11:

Corporal Smith enlisted in Illinois. In 2013, after serving four years of honorable service in the Marine Corps, he is about to separate and return home. Corporal Smith is interested in attending University of Illinois in Champaign and needs to determine his available education options.

Corporal Smith learns about the two federal GI Bills and the Illinois Veteran Grant (IVG) after reading this book. Corporal Smith needs to determine if he paid into MGIB, which would have been $100 per month for the first year of his enlistment to total $1,200. Corporal Smith believes he did but cannot remember for sure. Corporal Smith will double-check with IPAC to clarify but continues planning as if he did pay the $1,200 into MGIB.

Corporal Smith might also be eligible for IVG. Only the Illinois state VA can ultimately determine his eligibility, and he will need to verify with them if he will be able to use the benefit prior to following through with the details.

IVG will cover the cost of tuition and certain fees for eligible veterans at state-supported universities and community colleges within the state of Illinois. If Corporal Smith does rate IVG, he might do better financially by using it in tandem with MGIB, as opposed to opting for Post 9/11.

Here is the IVG eligibility list from the Illinois State VA (also at http://www2.illinois.gov/veterans/benefits/pages/education.aspx) that I reviewed with Corporal Smith (remember, things change!):

- Veteran must have received an honorable discharge.
- Veteran must have resided in Illinois six months prior to entering the service.
- Veteran must have completed a minimum of one full year of active duty in the U.S. Armed Forces (this includes veterans who were assigned to active duty in a foreign country in a time of hostilities in that country, regardless of length of service).
- Veteran must return to Illinois within six months of separation from the service.

Corporal Smith falls within the above-mentioned parameters, feels confident that he will rate the IVG, and proceeds accordingly.

Looking up the MHA stipend for the Post 9/11 GI Bill (at https://www.defensetravel.dod.mil/site/bahCalc.cfm), Corporal Smith finds the MHA stipend for the academic year 2013 is $1,047. This tool can also be found by visiting the main Post 9/11 GI Bill webpage (http://www.gibill.va.gov). Champaign, Illinois, is located in a rural, southern portion of the state; hence, the housing allowance under Post 9/11 is on the low side. Corporal Smith feels that this amount is on the low side and that he could do better if he elects to stay under MGIB, instead of choosing Post 9/11.

Here are his calculations:

- Post 9/11 MHA: $1,047
- MGIB payments (as of 2013–2014 school year): $1,564
- Corporal Smith will rate IVG, which will pay most of his public university's tuition and fees.
- If Corporal Smith pays the $600 Buy-Up to MGIB prior to separation, it will increase his monthly MGIB payments by an extra $150 per month, so his monthly take-home amount would be $1,714, or $667 more than the

$1,047 he would receive under Post 9/11. If none of the amounts change over the thirty-six months that Corporal Smith has allotted, he would take home $24,012 more under MGIB than he would under Post 9/11 over the course of the thirty-six months of benefits.

- One drawback is that IVG can be used for a master's degree as well. If Corporal Smith double-dips on his federal and state-based benefit at the same time, he may not retain any benefits that could have been used for graduate school. That is a personal decision.

Corporal Smith reviews his calculations and realizes that he still needs to verify his IVG with the Illinois state VA and his GI Bill eligibility with the federal VA. He also needs to contact the veterans' representatives (vet reps) at University of Illinois to discuss which GI Bill the veterans already attending the school have chosen and any recommendations that the vet reps may have for him. Corporal Smith must decide whether he minds depleting both of his benefits at the same time, since tapping into them simultaneously will result in that outcome.

In the case of Illinois veterans who meet IVG requirements, they must decide if the extra payoff they obtain by depleting both benefits at the same time is worth it. Many veterans may want to pursue a graduate degree with that benefit at a later date, and others may be more interested in maximizing their benefits immediately. Also remember that Corporal Smith is going to attend a school in a rural area. If you are from Illinois and elect an institution closer to Chicago, your MHA amount will be much higher than the listed amount for University of Illinois in Champaign. In this case, double-dipping is not necessary.

The second instance in which some veterans have opted for MGIB is for online-only school. Under the Post 9/11 GI Bill, veterans receive only $714.50 in MHA (as of academic year 2013–2014) for strictly online school, because you must attend a minimum of one face-to-face class every semester in order to rate the full MHA assigned to the ZIP code of the school. In a few cases, veterans who decide that they can only attend online school may do better by remaining under MGIB and paying the $600 Buy-Up prior to separation.

In the case of strictly online school, it is difficult to run numbers in this book because there are too many unknown factors. Examples of this include tuition charges, MHA attached to the school's ZIP code, and fluctuations in GI Bill payouts.

Here is a hypothetical example:

Corporal Smith decides to attend a fully online academic program. The cost of the school per credit hour is $250. He is taking two classes over an eight-week semester. The total cost for his two classes will be $1,500. The MHA for strictly online school at this point in time is $714.50 per month. Corporal Smith paid the $600 Buy-Up program at IPAC (Unit Diary entry) before separating. His combined monthly payout under MGIB and the Buy-Up program for academic year 2013–2014 is $1,714. In the span of his eight-week classes, he will take in $3,428. After paying his $1,500 bill for his two classes (two classes on an eight-week-semester schedule is considered full-time), he is left with $1,928. That is roughly $499 more than what he would take home if he had elected Post 9/11 and received only the $714.50 that is allotted for strictly online school ($1,924 − $1,429 = $499). MGIB, in this case, looks like the better choice.

Other state-based benefits can get a bit trickier. As of right now, only some states offer in-state tuition to out-of-state residents. The Student Veterans of America maintains a website where you can check to see if the state where you plan on attending school offers you this benefit (http://www.studentveterans.org/what-we-do/in-state-tuition.html). Some university systems will also grant in-state tuition for veterans. There are always qualifying criteria you must abide by, so, like I keep stating throughout this book, always check with the state VA or with the vet reps at the school to verify your eligibility.

As a veteran, it is important that you follow through with your own research on state and federal benefits. States are often updating and adding benefits for veterans. The monetary amounts attached to the federal GI Bills change as well. The only way to stay current with the information is to become fluent with the websites and check back regularly.

States That Offer In-State Tuition to Veterans

Here are the websites for the states that currently offer in-state residency to veterans. Some of these states offer other veteran benefits as well. There are specific steps (like registering to vote or getting a driver's license) tied into eligibility for the in-state tuition, and sometimes it is up to the school to participate. Check with the veterans' representatives at the institution you wish to attend to determine how to get going with the process for that particular state. Keep up to speed with states that change their legislation by checking the Student Veterans of America website (at http://www. studentveterans.org/what-we-do/in-state-tuition.html).

- Alabama (http://openstates.org/al/bills/2013rs/HB424/documents/ALD0 0016731/): In-state tuition for veterans who reside in Alabama and were honorably discharged within the five years immediately preceding their enrollment into a state institution of higher learning. Reservists and service-connected disabled veterans are eligible as well.
- Arizona (http://dvs.az.gov/tuition.aspx, (602) 255-3373): In-state tuition for veterans who registered to vote in the state and meet at least one of the following parameters: possess an Arizona driver license, have an Arizona motor vehicle registration, demonstrate employment history in Arizona, transfer their banking services to Arizona, change their permanent address on all pertinent records, or demonstrate other materials of whatever kind or source relevant to domicile or residency status.
- California (http://www.calvet.ca.gov/VetServices/Education.aspx, (916) 653-2573): Currently, the state of California offers honorary residency to veterans who were stationed in California for one year prior to separation from the military, separate, and stay in the state to attend an institution of higher education.
- Colorado (http://highered.colorado.gov/Finance/Residency/requirements. html, (303) 866-2723): In-state tuition for qualifying veterans and dependents. Veterans must be honorably discharged and maintain a permanent home in Colorado. Enlisted service members who are stationed in Colorado and receiving the resident student rate (themselves or their dependents) will be able to maintain that rate upon separation from the military if they continue to reside in the state.
- Florida (www.flsenate.gov/Session/Bill/2014/7015/BillText/er/PDF): In-state tuition for honorably discharged veterans at state community colleges, state colleges, and universities.
- Idaho (www.legislature.idaho.gov/legislation/2010/S1367.pdf, (208) 577-2310): In-state tuition for qualified veterans and qualifying dependents. Veterans must have served at least two years on active duty, have received an honorable discharge, and enter a public school within one year of separating from the service. Dependents must receive at least 50 percent of their support from the qualifying veteran.
- Illinois (http://studentveterans.org/media-news/press-releases/128-illinois -passes-in-state-tuition-for-veterans.html, http://www3.illinois.gov/Press

Releases/ShowPressRelease.cfm?SubjectID=3&RecNum=11434):   Recently passed by the governor; all veterans using the Post 9/11 GI Bill will
be billed as in-state residents at state-supported institutions.
- Indiana (www.in.gov/legislative/bills/2013/SE/SE0177.1.html): Veterans
  enrolled in undergraduate classes no more than twelve months after honorably separating from the armed forces or Indiana National Guard are eligible for in-state tuition.
- Kentucky   (http://cpe.ky.gov/policies/academicpolicies/residency.htm,
  (502) 573-1555): In-state tuition for qualifying veterans.
- Louisiana (http://legiscan.com/LA/text/HB435/id/649958): In-state tuition
  for veterans who served a minimum of two years on active duty and
  received an honorable discharge. Veterans who have been assigned service-connected disability ratings and are either already enrolled or applying for enrollment in a state institution are eligible as well.
- Maine   (www.mainelegislature.org/legis/bills/getDoc.asp?id=39934):
  Honorably discharged veterans enrolled in a program of education within
  the University of Maine system, the Maine community college system, or
  the Maritime Academy are eligible for in-state tuition.
- Maryland   (http://mgaleg.maryland.gov/webmga/frmStatutesText.aspx?
  article=ged&section=15-106.4&ext=html&session=2014RS&tab=
  subject5): In-state tuition for honorably discharged veterans of the armed
  forces. Veteran must reside in Maryland and attend a state institution of
  higher learning.
- Minnesota   (https://www.revisor.mn.gov/statutes/?id=197.775&format=
  pdf): In-state tuition at the undergraduate rate for veterans.
- Missouri (www.senate.mo.gov/13info/BTS_Web/Bill.aspx?SessionType=
  R&BillID=17138567): In-state tuition for veterans who received honorable or general discharges from the service. Benefit can be utilized at the
  state two-year or four-year institutions. Two-year institutions also offer
  the in-district rate.
- Nebraska   (http://nebraskalegislature.gov/FloorDocs/Current/PDF/Final/
  LB740.pdf): Honorably discharged veterans receive in-state tuition if
  more than two years has not passed since their date of separation from
  service. Dependents are eligible as well. Not applicable if the service
  member is eligible for the Yellow Ribbon Program.
- Nevada   (http://leg.state.nv.us/Session/77th2013/Bills/AB/AB260_EN.
  pdf): In-state tuition for veterans who were honorably discharged and

matriculated no more than two years after their date of separation from the armed forces.

- New Mexico (http://www.dvs.state.nm.us/benefits.html, (505) 827-6374): In-state tuition for qualified veterans, their spouses, and their children.
- North Dakota (www.legis.nd.gov/cencode/t15c10.pdf?20131106152541): In-state tuition for veterans who served 180 days or more on active duty and received an honorable discharge. Dependents who received transferred Post 9/11 benefits may also be eligible.
- Ohio (http://veteransaffairs.ohio.gov/, (614) 644-0898): In-state tuition for qualified veterans.
- Oregon (https://olis.leg.state.or.us/liz/2013R1/Measures/Text/HB2158/Enrolled): Honorably discharged veterans who establish a physical presence in Oregon within twelve months of enrolling in school may be eligible for in-state tuition and fees.
- South Dakota (http://legis.state.sd.us/statutes/DisplayStatute.aspx?Type=Statute&Statute=13-53-29.1): In-state tuition for honorably discharged veterans with at least ninety days of service.
- Tennessee (http://www.capitol.tn.gov/Bills/108/Bill/SB1433.pdf): In-state tuition for veterans discharged within two years and did not receive a dishonorable separation.
- Texas (http://www.statutes.legis.state.tx.us/Docs/ED/htm/ED.54.htm#54.241): In-state tuition for veterans who qualify for federal education benefits. Dependents may qualify as well.
- Utah (http://le.utah.gov/code/TITLE53B/pdf/53B08_010200.pdf, (801) 326-2372): In-state tuition for qualifying veterans at certain schools.
- Virginia (http://lis.virginia.gov/cgi-bin/legp604.exe?000+cod+23-7.4): Veterans released or discharged under conditions other than dishonorable are eligible for in-state tuition.
- Washington (http://apps.leg.wa.gov/documents/billdocs/2013-14/Pdf/Bills/Senate%20Passed%20Legislature/5318.PL.pdf): Veterans (and their dependents) who served a minimum of two years in the military and received an honorable discharge will be granted in-state tuition as long as they enroll in school within one year of their date of separation from the service.

A few state-based university systems across the country may also offer veterans in-state tuition without a state-based benefit in place. The following is a current list:

- University of Alaska school system: http://www.alaska.edu/bor/policy-regulations/
- Mississippi Institutions of Higher Learning: http://www.ihl.state.ms.us/board/downloads/policiesandbylaws.pdf
- University of Wisconsin school system: https://docs.legis.wisconsin.gov/statutes/statutes/36/27/2/b/4
- Kentucky Public Universities: http://www.lrc.ky.gov/record/11rs/HB425.htm
- University of Iowa school system: http://www.registrar.uiowa.edu/LinkClick.aspx?fileticket=EnXD7AdsnJ0%3d&tabid=94
- University System of Georgia: http://www.usg.edu/policymanual/section7/C453/
- University of Rhode Island: http://www.uri.edu/home/campus/
- University of Delaware: http://www.udel.edu/aboutus/

Many institutions of higher learning have adopted scholarships for disabled veterans. For example, the University of Idaho has the Operation Education scholarship that may provide financial assistance for eligible service-connected disabled veterans and their spouses (http://www.uidaho.edu/operationeducation). Check with the institutions you are interested in attending to obtain information regarding policies or programs that may benefit you.

The following are states with state-based education benefits at this time. Most of the information is taken directly from the state VA websites.

Alabama

http://www.va.state.al.us/scholarship.htm

Benefit

Purple Heart (PH) recipients may be eligible to have tuition and fees waived for undergraduate studies.

State residents with service-connected disability ratings of 20 percent or higher may qualify for his or her:

- Spouse: three standard academic years without payment of tuition, mandatory textbooks, or instructional fees at a state institution of higher learning, or for a prescribed technical course not to exceed twenty-seven months of training at a state institution.

- Dependent children: five standard academic years or part-time equivalent at any Alabama state-supported institution of higher learning or a state-supported technical school without payment of any tuition, mandatory textbooks, or instructional fees. Dependent children must start school prior to age twenty-six.

Eligibility and residency requirements for veterans:

- Must have honorably served at least ninety days of continuous active federal military service during wartime, or honorably discharged by reason of service-connected disability after serving less than ninety days of continuous active federal military service during wartime.
- Permanent civilian resident of the State of Alabama for at least one year immediately prior to (1) the initial entry into active military service or (2) any subsequent period of military service in which a break (one year or more) in service occurred and the Alabama civilian residency was established. Permanently service-connected veterans rated at 100 percent who did not enter service from Alabama may qualify but must first establish at least five years of permanent residency in Alabama prior to application.

Note: If you are a veteran with a PH and MGIB, you may want to stay on MGIB instead of electing Post 9/11.

The following subsection is a breakdown of current payout under MGIB versus Post 9/11 with a veteran using his or her Alabama state benefit under MGIB at a community college.

Northeast Alabama Community College

MGIB currently pays out $1,564/month + $600 (Buy-Up) = $1,714/month
Total for four months = $6,856
MHA under Post 9/11 $957 × four months = $3,828

Veterans who qualify for the state-based PH waiver earn $3,028 more in four months under MGIB than if they opted for Post 9/11. Remember that the state pays the school tuition in this case.

California

http://www.calvet.ca.gov/VetServices/Education.aspx

Benefit

> Dependent children tuition waiver at state-supported schools for service-connected disabled veterans

There are four different pathways for eligibility for the California State benefit. They can get confusing. Mainly, they are Medal of Honor recipients and their children, National Guard, children of veterans with service-connected disabilities (the most common category), and spouses (veteran is totally disabled, or whose death was service connected). Let's discuss the most common category: children. California veterans who rate a 0 percent disability rating or higher may qualify for their children to receive waivers of tuition at state community colleges and universities. Please note that a 0 percent disability rating is an actual rating. Fees for books, housing, parking, and so on are not included in the waiver. The state of California does not care where you enlisted. If you separate, have a service-connected disability, and become a California resident, you may be eligible.

This is a great way to get your children's college covered. Many veterans use the benefit to send their children to state schools to pursue higher education and not worry about the bills. The universities in the state are used to children using this benefit, and the veterans' representatives at the institutions know how to facilitate it for dependent children.

To read a more thorough breakdown of eligibility, check the website (http://www.calvet.ca.gov/Files/VetServices/Veterans_Resource_Book.pdf).

Eligibility and residency requirements for children for the most common pathway:

- Must make less than $11,945 per year.
- Must meet in-state residency requirements determined by school.
- Provide proof of relationship to the veteran.

Benefit

> In-state tuition for veterans; must be stationed in California for one year prior to separation, separate in the state, and remain in California for school
> http://www.calvet.ca.gov/VetServices/NonResFeeWaiver.aspx

Connecticut

http://www.ct.gov/ctva/cwp/view.asp?A=2014&Q=290874

Benefit

Tuition waivers at Connecticut state community colleges and state colleges and universities for eligible veterans

Only the cost of tuition is waived. Other charges, such as books, student fees, and parking, are not waived. Students must be matriculated into a degree program.

Eligibility and residency requirements for veterans:

- Veteran must be honorably discharged.
- Must have served at least ninety days of active military duty during war.
- Must be a resident of Connecticut at least one year prior to enrolling in college.
- Must be a resident of Connecticut at the time he or she applies for the state benefit.

Florida

http://floridavets.org/?page_id=60

Benefit

Waiver of undergraduate-level tuition at state universities and community colleges for recipients of the PH and other combat-related decorations superior in precedence to the PH. Waiver covers 110 percent of the required credit hours for the degree or certificate.

Eligibility and residency requirements:

- Veteran must be admitted as a part- or full-time student in a course of study leading to a degree or certificate.
- Must have been a Florida State resident at the time the military action that resulted in the awarding of the PH (or other award) took place and must currently be a Florida State resident.
- Must submit DD-214 documenting PH to school.

Illinois

http://www2.illinois.gov/veterans/benefits/Pages/education.aspx

Benefit

The Illinois Veterans' Grant (IVG): IVG is a tuition (and certain fees) waiver for undergraduate and graduate studies at state-supported institutions for veterans who served during a time of hostilities.

Eligibility and residency requirements:

- Veteran must have received an honorable discharge.
- Must have resided in Illinois six months prior to entering the military.
- Have served a minimum of one year on active duty with the Armed Forces or was assigned to active duty in a foreign country in a time of hostilities in that country, regardless of length of service.
- Must return to Illinois within six months of separation from the military.

Many Illinois veterans choose to stay under MGIB as opposed to Post 9/11 to fully maximize dollar amounts under their available benefits. If they plan on attending school in a rural area—for example, University of Illinois in Champaign—double-dipping on MGIB and IVG can produce more money on a monthly basis. If you do this, be aware that you will be depleting both state and federal benefits at the same time. That means that you may not have any benefits left for a master's degree at a later date.

If the school you choose is located in a rural area, and the MHA on Post 9/11 is significantly less than the maxed-out MGIB amount (currently $1,564 per month), then double-dipping will be more beneficial.

Here is an example:

Recently, Lance Corporal Stevens went to University of Illinois in Champaign. The MHA for the 2013–2014 school year was $1,047 (http://inquiry.vba.va.gov/weamspub/buildViewOrg.do). Lance Corporal Stevens was an Illinois state resident at his time of enlistment and qualified for the Illinois Veteran Grant. He elected to stay under MGIB, and went to pay the Buy-Up at IPAC (Unit Diary entry) prior to his EAS date.

The Buy-Up option under MGIB increases the monthly payments and must be paid while still on active duty. Buy-Up can be paid in different increments, but I recommend that the maximum of $600 be paid in order to get the maximum monthly increase of $150. After paying the full Buy-Up amount, the MGIB monthly payments are increased to $1,714. Remember that these amounts will change yearly as the cost of living adjustment (COLA) increases.

Lance Corporal Stevens will double-dip off IVG and MGIB. IVG will pay the school tuition, and he will collect $1,714 per month under MGIB as opposed to $1,047 per month under the MHA on Post 9/11. That is a difference of $667 per month. Over the course of a nine-month school year, the veteran earns an extra $6,003. A much better deal all around! But do not forget that once you select Post 9/11, you can never return to MGIB, so make an educated decision.

Benefit

> Children of Veterans Scholarship: http://www.osfa.uiuc.edu/aid/scholarships/waivers_COV.html

Each county in the state is authorized one scholarship yearly at the University of Illinois for children of veterans of World War I, World War II, the Korean War, the Vietnam Conflict, Operation Enduring Freedom, or Operation Iraqi Freedom. Children of deceased and disabled veterans are considered priority. These children can receive four consecutive years tuition free (undergraduate, graduate, or professional studies) at the University of Illinois (Urbana-Champaign, Chicago Health Sciences Center, or Springfield Campus).

Indiana

> http://www.in.gov/dva/2378.htm

Benefit

> Indiana Purple Heart Recipients receive free tuition at the resident tuition rate for 124 semester credit hours at state-supported postsecondary schools for undergraduate study only.

> Eligibility and residency requirements:

- Entered service from a permanent home address in Indiana.
- Received the PH.
- Received an honorable discharge.
- Veteran entered service prior to June 30, 2011.

Be aware that the law changed in 2011. Here is the difference between the old and new laws.

Under the old law, for a veteran who entered service *prior to* June 30, 2011:

- Free resident tuition for the children of disabled veterans, or PH recipients.
- Benefit includes 124 semester hours of tuition and mandatory fees at the undergraduate rate.
- Benefit can be used for graduate school, but the difference between the undergraduate and graduate rate is the responsibility of the student.

Eligibility and residency requirements:

- Biological (adopted by age twenty-four) and legally adopted children of eligible disabled Indiana veterans.
- Child must produce a copy of birth certificate or adoption papers.
- Veteran must have served during a period of wartime.
- Veteran must have been a resident of Indiana for a minimum of three consecutive years at some point in his or her lifetime.
- Must rate a service-connected disability (or have died a service-connected death), or received the PH (demonstration of proof is necessary for either).

Under the new law, for a veteran who entered service *on or after* July 1, 2011:

- Free resident tuition for the children of disabled veterans or PH recipients.
- Benefit includes 124 semester hours of tuition and mandatory fees for undergraduate study only.
- Benefit is based on the level of disability the veteran rates (see below).
- Student must maintain a mandatory minimum GPA (see below).
- The program limits the student to eight years.

Eligibility and residency requirements:

- Biological (adopted by age eighteen) and legally adopted children of eligible disabled Indiana veterans.
- Child must produce a copy of birth certificate or adoption papers.
- Veteran must have served during a period of wartime.

- Must rate a service-connected disability (or have died a service-connected death) or have received the PH (demonstration of proof is necessary for either).
- Student must apply prior to turning thirty-two years old.

Disability rating pro-rated schedule for tuition (taken directly from the website):

- Children of veterans rated 80 percent service-connected disabled or higher by the VA or whose veteran parent is or was a recipient of the PH medal will receive 100 percent fee remission.
- Children of veterans rated less than 80 percent service-connected disabled will receive 20 percent fee remission, plus the disability rating of the veteran.
- If the disability rating of the veteran changes after the beginning of the academic semester, quarter, or other period, the change in the disability rating shall be applied starting with the immediately following academic semester, quarter, or other period.

GPA requirements:

- First-year student must maintain satisfactory academic progress.
- Second-, third-, and fourth-year students must maintain a minimum cumulative GPA of 2.5.

Maryland

http://www.mdva.state.md.us/state/scholarships.html

Benefit

Edward T. Conroy Memorial Scholarship

Aid for qualifying veterans or children of veterans to attend part-time or full-time Maryland state school (community college, university, or private career school). Benefit works for undergraduate and graduate school. It is not based on economic need. The award is for tuition and fees, but it may not exceed $10,100, whichever is less. The award works for five years at the full-time attendance rate, or eight years at part-time. More detailed information can be found at www.mhec.state.md.us/financialAid/COARenewal/2013-

2014/2013-2014%20conroy%20conditions%20of%20award%20renewal.
pdf.
Eligibility and residency requirements:

- Children of veterans who have died, or who are 100 percent disabled as a result of military service.
- Veterans who have a 25 percent or greater disability rating with the VA and have exhausted federal veterans' education benefits.
- Must be a Maryland resident.

Benefit

Veterans of the Afghanistan and Iraq Conflicts (VAIC) Scholarship Program

The award is 50 percent of tuition and fees and room and board at the in-state, undergraduate rate at a school within the University of Maryland system (UMUC and University of Maryland, Baltimore, are exempt from this award). The award shall not exceed $10,400 for the 2013–2014 school year. All undergraduate majors are eligible. This award works for five years at the full-time attendance rate, or eight years at part-time. Students must maintain a minimum 2.5 GPA.
Eligibility and residency requirements:

- Must have served in Afghanistan (minimum sixty days) on or after October 24, 2001, or in Iraq on or after March 19, 2003 (minimum sixty days).
- Be on active duty or a veteran (honorable discharge), or the son, daughter, or spouse of the aforementioned categories.
- Must attend school part- or full-time and be degree seeking.
- Supporting documentation of relationship to veteran is necessary (birth certificate or marriage certificate).
- Supporting documentation of active-duty status (orders) or DD-214 necessary.
- Applicant must be a resident of Maryland (active-duty military stationed in the state at the time of application qualify).

Massachusetts

http://www.mass.gov/veterans/education/financial-assistance/tuition-waivers.html

Benefit

Waiver of full or partial tuition at state institutions of higher education on a space-available basis for undergraduate study. (Fees are not included and can be very high.) Graduate school waivers are dependent upon each university. Waivers are for degree or certificate programs.

Eligibility and residency requirements:

- Must be a resident of the state for at least one year prior to the start of the school year.
- Must not be in default of any federal or state loans or financial aid.
- Served a minimum of ninety days and received an honorable discharge.
- Maintain a minimum of three undergraduate credits per semester and make satisfactory academic progress.

Minnesota

http://mn.gov/mdva/resources/education/minnesotagibill.jsp
(800) 657-3866

Benefit

A maximum payment of $1,000 per semester for full-time students and $500 per semester for part-time students. No more than $10,000 per lifetime. Eligible veterans pursuing OJT or apprenticeship programs can receive up to $2,000 per fiscal year.

Eligibility and residency requirements:

- Veteran must be a Minnesota resident, under the age of 62, and enrolled in a Minnesota institution.
- Must have received an honorable discharge.
- Spouse of a disabled veteran (total and permanent) or surviving spouse or child of a veteran who died as a result of his or her service (must be eligible to receive benefits under Chapter 33/35).
- OJT and apprenticeships must be completed with eligible employers (http://www.doli.state.mn.us/Appr.asp).
- Training must be documented, be reported, and last for at least six months.

Veterans must reapply every year. More information and important links can be found on the website.

Missouri

http://www.dhe.mo.gov/files/moretheroesact.pdf

Benefit

Missouri Returning Heroes' Education Act limits Missouri institutions of higher education from charging eligible veterans more than $50 per credit hour.

Eligibility and residency requirements:

- Received an honorable discharge.
- Served in an armed combat zone for more than thirty days after September 11, 2001.
- Veteran was a Missouri resident when he or she entered the service.
- Must enroll in an undergraduate degree-seeking program.
- Must maintain a minimum 2.5 GPA every semester.

Note: Missouri residents who qualify for this benefit and MGIB should run the numbers before electing Post 9/11. Many of the veterans I counsel choose to stay under MGIB as opposed to Post 9/11 to fully maximize their dollars under their available benefits.

Speak to a counselor at your closest education center aboard the base, or contact the veterans' representatives at your chosen school for advice. Remember, once you select Post 9/11, you can never return to MGIB, so make an educated decision.

Example: Staff Sergeant Carlson meets the eligibility requirements as listed above. He will attend Three Rivers Community College in Poplar Bluff, Missouri. The housing allowance under Post 9/11 is $999 per month. The tuition per semester will be $750 (for fifteen credit hours) under his state-based benefit. If he elects to remain under MGIB, he needs to pay the Buy-Up at IPAC (Unit Diary entry) prior to his EAS date, and then he will receive $1,714 per month. After paying his tuition the first month, he will have $964 remaining, but for every month after that he will receive $1,714 for the rest of the semester. That means $715 more per month than if he had elected Post 9/11. The process would repeat itself every semester. Veterans who elect this option must remember that the book stipend is only received under Post 9/11.

Let's run the numbers:

- Tuition per semester: $750 (verify that you will not need to pay any other large fees).
- MGIB with Buy-Up: $6,856 (based on a four-month semester).
- Minus the tuition for the semester: $6,106.
- Minus the book stipend that would be received under Post 9/11: $5,606.
- Post 9/11 MHA for the school $999 per month: $3,996.
- Including the books and supplies stipend under 9/11 for the semester: $4,496.
- This amounts to $1,110 more per semester if the veteran decides to remain under MGIB and also qualifies for the state-based benefit.
- Remember that under MGIB, you must verify that you are attending school each month.
- He elected to stay under MGIB, and he paid the Buy-Up at IPAC (Unit Diary entry) prior to his EAS date.

Explanation of the MGIB Buy-Up: The Buy-Up option under MGIB increases the monthly payments and must be paid while still on active duty. Buy-Up can be paid in different increments, but I recommend the maximum of $600 be paid in order to get the maximum monthly increase of $150. After paying the full Buy-Up amount, the MGIB monthly payments are increased to $1,714. Remember that these amounts will change yearly as the COLA increases.

Always remember to verify eligibility for the state-based benefits and call the veterans' representatives at the school before making any final decisions.

Montana

http://www.montana.edu/veteran/honor_dis.shtml

Benefit

Tuition waivers for eligible wartime veterans who have exhausted all federal education benefits. The award works for undergraduate programs of study for a maximum of twelve semesters. Veteran must make satisfactory academic progress.

Eligibility and residency requirements:

- Must be a state resident.
- Received an honorable discharge.
- Veteran has not already received a bachelor's degree.
- Served in a combat theatre in Afghanistan or Iraq after September 11, 2001 (must have received one of the following: Global War on Terrorism Expeditionary Medal, Afghanistan Campaign Medal, or Iraq Campaign Medal).

New York

http://veterans.ny.gov/content/veterans-tuition-awards

Benefit

Veterans' tuition awards are available for students attending undergraduate or graduate degree-granting schools, or vocational training programs at the part- or full-time rate.

This award covers the full cost of the undergraduate tuition for New York residents at the State University of New York (SUNY) or the actual amount of the tuition (whatever is the lesser charge).

"Full-time" is defined as twelve or more credits per semester (a maximum of eight semesters for undergraduate study and six for graduate study). "Part-time" is at least three, but fewer than twelve, credits per semester (within the same timeframes).

The benefit was set at a maximum of $5,595 for the 2012–2013 school year. Veterans who qualify for the state benefit and MGIB may be able to "double-dip" (there is no "double-dipping" under Post 9/11, unless the veteran is not eligible for 100 percent).

Vocational programs need to be approved by the State of New York and must be at least 320 clock hours in duration.

Eligibility and residency requirements:

- Must be a New York State resident.
- Certain eligible periods of service pertain (mainly if you served in hostilities after February 28, 1961, as evidenced by receipt of an Armed Forces Expeditionary Medal, Navy Expeditionary Medal, or Marine Corps Expeditionary Medal).

- Must be matriculated in an undergraduate or graduate degree-granting institution in New York State or in an approved vocational training program in New York State.

Benefit

Military Service Recognition Scholarship: Financial aid for qualifying veterans and dependents of veterans. The award is a maximum of four years (five for approved five-year programs) of full-time study at the undergraduate level, and it works at SUNY or City University of New York (CUNY) schools for the actual tuition and mandatory fees, plus room and board (on campus) and books and supplies. Those who attend school off-campus will receive an allowance. Private school attendees will receive a sum equal to the public school costs.

Eligibility and residency requirements:

- New York residents who died or became severely and permanently disabled (verify degree with the state) while participating in hostilities, or in training for duty in a combat theater.
- Must have occurred on or after August 2, 1990.

North Carolina

http://www.doa.state.nc.us/vets/scholarshipclasses.aspx

Benefit

Scholarships for dependent children of veterans who rate a minimum of 20 percent disability and served during wartime, or received the Purple Heart

Maximum of one hundred awards per year.

The award is for eight semesters completed within eight years. It covers tuition, an allowance for room and board, and exemption from certain mandatory fees at public, community, and technical colleges and institutions, or $4,500 per academic year at private schools.

Eligibility and residency requirements:

- Natural and adopted (prior to age fifteen) children of qualifying veterans.
- Must be under the age of twenty-five.

- Upon submission of application, student must be a resident of North Carolina.
- Veteran must have entered service in North Carolina, or the applicant must have been born in North Carolina and maintained continuous residency in the state.

Oregon

www.oregon.gov/odva/BENEFITS/Pages/OregonEducationBenefit.aspx

Benefit

The Oregon Veteran Educational Aid Program

Financial aid for veterans who have exhausted all federal education benefits. The maximum award is thirty-six months (award months equal months of service) of $150 per month for full-time students, or $100 per month for part-time students. Face-to-face classes, home study, vocational training, licenses, and certificates from accredited Oregon academic institutions are eligible.

Benefits are paid while pursuing classroom instruction, home study courses, vocational training, licensing, and certificates from accredited Oregon educational institutions.

Eligibility and residency requirements:

- Must have served on active duty a minimum of ninety days and received an honorable discharge.
- Be a resident of Oregon.
- Served after June 30, 1958.

Puerto Rico

http://www.nasdva.com/puertorico.html

Benefit

For those attending University of Puerto Rico and its regional colleges, free tuition for veterans who have exhausted federal benefits before completing a degree.

Eligibility and residency requirement: Verify qualifying criteria with the institutions.

South Carolina

http://www.govoepp.state.sc.us/va/benefits.html#ed_assis

Benefit

Free tuition for children of veterans who have been awarded the PH for wounds received in combat. The award can be used at state-supported schools or technical education institutions.

Eligibility and residency requirements:

- Veteran must have been a resident at time of entry into the military and throughout the service period (or veteran has been a resident of South Carolina for a minimum of one year and still resides in the state).
- Veteran was honorably discharged.
- Served during a war period.
- Student must be twenty-six years old or younger.

South Dakota

http://vetaffairs.sd.gov/benefits/State/State%20Education%20Programs .aspx

Benefit

Free tuition for eligible veterans who have exhausted all federal education benefits they were eligible to receive

The award is pro-rated on the veteran's qualifying military service (one month for each qualified month of service, for a maximum of four years). Veteran has twenty years from the end date of a qualifying service period to use the entitlement.

Eligibility and residency requirements:

- Veteran must be a resident of the state and qualify for resident tuition.
- Received an honorable discharge.
- Received a U.S. campaign or service medal for participating in combat operations outside of the United States (e.g., an Armed Forces Expeditionary medal).
- Veteran has a 10 percent (or more) disability rating with the VA.

Tennessee

http://www.tn.gov/sos/rules/1640/1640-01-22.20090529.pdf

Benefit

The Helping Heroes Grant for Veterans is available yearly to a maximum of 375 qualifying veterans.

The $1,000 per semester award is given on a first-come, first-served basis to students completing a minimum of twelve credit hours per semester. The award can be applied for until the eighth anniversary of the veteran's separation date, or when the student has received the award for a total of eight semesters.

Eligibility and residency requirements:

1. Be a Tennessee resident for one year prior to application.
2. Be admitted to an eligible institution of higher education for an associate or bachelor's degree.
3. Receive an honorable discharge.
4. Veteran received the Iraq Campaign Medal, Afghanistan Campaign Medal, or Global War on Terrorism Expeditionary Medal on or after September 1, 2001.
5. Not be in default on any federal student aid programs or Tennessee student financial aid programs.
6. Veteran does not have a bachelor's degree already.
7. Veteran is not in jail—that's right . . . you heard me (stated as so on the website).

Texas

http://veterans.portal.texas.gov/en/Pages/education.aspx

Benefit

Hazlewood tuition waivers at state institutions

A list of eligible schools can be found at http://www.collegeforalltexans.com/index.cfm?objectID=8F88F7F2-A11A-B69F-5E25D9D6F972DAE4&audience=military, under the "Public School" list. The award covers tuition, dues, fees, and other required charges up to 150 semester hours. The award will not cover room and board, books, student services fees, or deposit fees.

The waiver can be used for undergraduate and graduate classes. Teacher certification fees, aircraft flight-training courses, and distance-learning classes may also be covered (verify with the school).

Eligibility and residency requirements:

1. At the time of entry into the military was a Texas state resident, designated Texas as a home of record, or entered the service in Texas.
2. Veteran served a minimum of 181 days of active duty.
3. Received an honorable discharge (and provides proof of this fact).
4. Exhausted Post 9/11 GI Bill benefits.
5. Veteran is not in default on state-guaranteed student loans.
6. Must reside in Texas during the semester the exemption is being claimed (this rule started in the fall of 2011).

Note: Veterans are not able to "double-dip" with Post 9/11 and Hazlewood at the same time. Texas schools maintain a great amount of control over Hazlewood Act usage at their institutions. In most cases, veterans stay with Post 9/11. The Hazlewood Act's goal is to step in and cover tuition at state-supported institutions if an eligible individual runs out of GI Bill benefit. Always contact the vet reps at your institution of choice prior to making any final decisions.

Benefit

Legacy Program: http://www.tvc.texas.gov/Hazlewood-Act.aspx?CFID=
9607034&CFTOKEN=43720648

Children may be eligible to have unused Hazlewood benefits transferred to them. The award can only be used at state-supported institutions. A list of eligible schools can be found on http://collegeforalltexans.com/index.cfm?ObjectID=D57D0AC5-AB2D-EFB0-FC201080B528442A, under the "Public School" list. The award covers tuition, dues, fees, and other required charges up to 150 semester hours. The award will not cover room and board, books, student services fees, or deposit fees.

Eligibility and residency requirements:

1. Veteran was a Texas state resident when he or she entered the military, designated Texas as Home of Record, or entered the service in Texas.
2. Child must be the biological child, stepchild, or adopted child, or be claimed as a dependent in the current or previous tax year.

3. Be under the age of twenty-five at the beginning of any term for which the benefit is being claimed (some exemptions may apply).
4. Make satisfactory academic progress.
5. Provide proof of veteran's honorable discharge.

Benefit

Combat Tuition Exemption

Dependent children of service members deployed in combat zones receive tuition waivers (fees not exempted).

Eligibility and residency requirements:

1. Child must be a resident of Texas or entitled to receive the in-state tuition rate (dependents of military personnel stationed in Texas).
2. Must be enrolled during the time the service member is deployed in a combat zone.
3. If an out-of-state resident, the child may need to provide a copy of parent's orders.

Utah

http://veterans.utah.gov/state-benefits/

Benefit

PH recipients are eligible for tuition waivers at state schools.

The award works for undergraduate and graduate programs. Veterans who were eligible for this benefit should be able to complete a bachelor's and master's degree with little or no debt upon completion.

Eligibility and residency requirements:

1. Show proof of PH.
2. Be a Utah state resident.

Virgin Islands

http://www.militaryvi.org/benefits/

Benefit

Free tuition is offered for attendance at local public educational institutions and at the University of the Virgin Islands.

This program is for veterans who entered the Armed Forces while residing in the Virgin Islands. Contact the schools for more information.

Washington State

http://apps.leg.wa.gov/RCW/default.aspx?cite=28B.15.621

Benefit

Tuition waivers at state schools for undergraduate education for up to two hundred quarter credits (or equivalent semester credits). Waiver may be full or partial.

Some schools offer the waiver for graduate programs (check with your institution). Full- or part-time enrollment is eligible. The award may work at some private institutions. Be aware that the tuition may not be fully covered. Eligibility and residency requirements:

1. Must make satisfactory academic progress.
2. Must have served in a war or conflict fought on foreign soil or in international waters or in another location in support of those serving on foreign soil or in international waters.
3. Received an honorable discharge.
4. Be a resident of the state.

West Virginia

http://www.veterans.wv.gov/Pages/default.aspx

Benefit

West Virginia Veteran's Re-Education Scholarship Program

Eligible veterans can receive $500 per term (part-time students: $250). Amount cannot exceed a total of $1,500 per academic year. Program funding may be used to cover professional exam costs as well. Eligible veterans may use the scholarship in tandem with the Workforce Investment Act (WIA) and/or Trade Adjustment Act (TAA) if program cost exceeds the amount allocated under the latter two programs.

Eligibility and residency requirements:

1. Veteran must be a resident of the state.
2. Received an honorable discharge.
3. Served 181 consecutive days on active duty.
4. Eligible for Pell Grant or unemployed.
5. Veteran has exhausted all federal GI Bill money possibilities (including Vocational Rehabilitation, if eligible).

Wisconsin

http://www.wisvets.com/wisgibill

Benefit

Wisconsin GI Bill tuition remission benefit program (WI GI Bill)

Remission of tuition and fees at state institutions (University of Wisconsin and Wisconsin Technical Colleges) for eligible veterans and dependents. The award is good for a maximum of eight semesters (or 128 semester credits), undergraduate and graduate education, and professional programs. There are no income restrictions or delimiting periods. Many fees are not covered, such as books, meals, room and board, and online fees. This award cannot be combined with federal benefits.

Eligibility and residency requirements:

1. Veteran must have served since September 10, 2001, and entered the service from Wisconsin.
2. Must apply for Post 9/11 GI Bill benefits first, if eligible. (*Note*: Talk to an education counselor or the veterans' representatives before you elect which GI Bill you will use!)
3. Children and spouses of veterans with a combined rating of 30 percent or greater from the VA may be eligible for the award.
4. Child must be the biological child, stepchild, or adopted child, or any other child who is a member of the veteran's household.
5. Child must be at least seventeen but no older than twenty-six, and must be a resident of the state.
6. Spouse must be a resident of the state for tuition purposes.

7. Spouse has ten years from the date of the veteran's VA rating to use the benefit.

The most clearly written information on eligibility for the state education benefits can be found on the website (see http://dva.state.wi.us/WebForms/WDVA_B0105_Wisconsin_Tuition_Programs_WI_GI_Bill_Color.pdf).

The State of Wisconsin does not allow veterans to double-dip on federal and state-based benefits. However, if veterans paid into MGIB and if the MHA under Post 9/11 at the school they want to attend is less than what they would have received under MGIB, the school will reimburse the veteran for the difference. Talk to the veterans' representatives at the institutions for more information.

Benefit

Veterans Education Reimbursement (http://www.WisVets.com/VetEd)

Reimbursement grant program. Reimburses veteran after successful completion of coursework (University of Wisconsin locations, Wisconsin Technical Colleges, or a private institution of higher education in Wisconsin or Minnesota) at the undergraduate level only. Reimbursement is pro-rated based on aggregate length of qualifying active-duty service. Veterans with a minimum of 30 percent of qualifying disability from the VA are reimbursed at 100 percent.

Eligibility and residency requirements:

1. Veteran entered active duty as a Wisconsin resident, or lived in Wisconsin for twelve months prior to entering the service.
2. If veteran was discharged more than ten years ago, only reimbursement at the part-time rate is possible.
3. Must exhaust all other benefits first (including Wisconsin State GI Bill).
4. Maximum income limit applies (annual income of veteran and spouse cannot exceed $50,000, plus $1,000 for each dependent beyond two). Provide proof of income (adjusted gross income [AGI] from the current tax return).
5. Must not already possess a bachelor's degree.
6. Must not be delinquent on child support payments.
7. Must maintain a 2.0 GPA.

Wyoming

https://sites.google.com/a/wyo.gov/veteranseducation/home/state-tuition-assistance

Benefit

Free tuition and fees for overseas combat veterans

The award can be used at the University of Wyoming and the state community colleges. Eligible veterans can receive ten semesters of schooling through this benefit.

Eligibility and residency requirements:

1. Veteran must have had residency in state for a minimum of one year prior to entering service.
2. Home of residence on DD-214 states Wyoming.
3. Must have an honorable discharge.
4. Received the Armed Forces Expeditionary Medal or campaign medal for service in any conflict in a foreign country (list of qualifying medals found at http://www.communitycolleges.wy.edu/Data/Sites/1/commissionFiles/Programs/Veteran/_doc/expeditionary-medal-list--2-jul-07.pdf).
5. Maintains a 2.0 GPA.
6. Veteran has eight years from date of acceptance into program to use.
7. State-based education benefits based on severe levels of disability/or death.

Other State Benefits

There are other states besides those listed above that offer education benefits for spouses and/or children. In the case of these states, the veteran must be severely and permanently disabled or have died while on active-duty service (in many cases, in combat or combat-related situations). I am not going to cover the specific details of these benefits, but below you will find a list of the states that offer this benefit and the links to their websites.

Alabama: http://www.va.state.al.us/laws.htm#GIBILL
Alaska: http://www.veterans.alaska.gov/state_benefits.htm
Arkansas: http://www.veterans.arkansas.gov/benefits.html#edu
California: http://www.cdva.ca.gov/VetServices/CollegeFeeWaiver.aspx

Delaware: http://veteransaffairs.delaware.gov/veterans_benefits.shtml

Florida: http://floridavets.org/?page_id=60

Iowa: http://www.in.gov/dva/2378.htm

Kentucky: http://veterans.ky.gov/Benefits/Documents/KDVAInfoBookletIssueAugust2010.pdf

Louisiana: http://vetaffairs.la.gov/Programs/Education.aspx

Maine: http://www.maine.gov/dvem/bvs/VDEB_2.pdf

Maryland: http://veterans.maryland.gov/wp-content/uploads/sites/2/2013/10/MDBenefitsGuide.pdf

Massachusetts: www.mass.gov/veterans/education/for-family/mslf.html

Michigan: http://www.michigan.gov/dmva/0,4569,7-126-2362-305076--,00.html

Minnesota: http://www.mdva.state.mn.us/education/SurvivingSpouse DependentInformationSheet.pdf

Missouri: http://mvc.dps.mo.gov/docs/veterans-benefits-guide.pdf

Montana: http://data.opi.mt.gov/bills/mca/20/25/20-25-421.htm, http://wsd.dli.mt.gov/veterans/vetstatebenefits.asp

Nebraska: http://www.vets.state.ne.us/waiver.html

New Hampshire: http://www.nh.gov/nhveterans/benefits/education.htm

New Jersey: http://www.state.nj.us/military/veterans/programs.html

New Mexico: http://www.dvs.state.nm.us/benefits.html

New York: http://www.veterans.ny.gov/content/regents-awards-children-deceased-disabled-veterans

North Carolina: http://www.doa.nc.gov/vets/benefitslist.aspx?pid=scholarships

North Dakota: http://www.nd.gov/veterans/education/dependents.html

Ohio: https://www.ohiohighered.org/ohio-war-orphans

Oregon: http://www.ous.edu/stucoun/prospstu/vb

Pennsylvania: http://www.portal.state.pa.us/portal/server.pt/community/veterans_benefits/11386/disabled_benefits/567417, www.pheaa.org/funding-opportunities/other-educational-aid/postsecondary-educational-gratuity.shtml

South Carolina: http://www.govoepp.state.sc.us/va/documents/ftapp.pdf

South Dakota: http://mva.sd.gov/vet_benefits_info.html#Free+Tuition+for+Veterans

Tennessee: http://www.state.tn.us/veteran/state_benifits/dep_tuition.html

Texas: http://www.tvc.texas.gov/Hazlewood-Act.aspx

Utah: http://veterans.utah.gov/homepage/stateBenefits/index.html#scott
   blundell
Virginia: http://www.dvs.virginia.gov/veterans-benefits.shtml
Washington: http://www.dva.wa.gov/dependentstuitionwaiver.html
Wisconsin: http://dva.state.wi.us/Ben-education.asp#Tuition
West Virginia: http://www.veterans.wv.gov/assistance/Pages/default.aspx
Wyoming: https://sites.google.com/a/wyo.gov/wyomingmilitarydepart-
   ment/veterans-commission/veterans-benefits/vet-tuition

FEDERAL STUDENT AID

Free Application for Federal Student Aid (FAFSA^{SM})

http://www.fafsa.ed.gov/

TA money and GI Bills are a source of funding, but they are not the only source available. Active-duty and veteran service members can apply for Federal Student Aid and should be encouraged to do so, in order to cover any extra costs they are unable to get funded. For example, TA cannot cover books or supplies. Under the Post 9/11 GI Bill, if a student attends school full-time, he or she will receive $1,000 per academic year toward books and supplies. In most cases, this is not enough to cover book expenses. Federal Student Aid is a viable option to help in these circumstances.

Student aid can come from the U.S. federal government, states, schools, and nonprofit organizations. Student aid money is usually provided on a first-come, first-served basis. Most students elect to apply for Federal Student Aid through the U.S. Department of Education, but not everyone qualifies. Prior to applying for Federal Student Aid, it is important to understand what it is, how it works, and what you would want to accept.

Federal Student Aid comes in three forms: work study, loans, and grants. Work study might be an option upon separation from the service but is not a feasible option for active-duty service members. The VA work-study program is a great option for veterans who are interested in making extra money while attending school and keeping their work activity on their résumé full at the same time. More information on VA work studies can be found later in this book (see chapter 13).

Active-duty and veteran students using their GI Bills should not require loans in most cases. In fact, it is best to avoid them at all costs. Typically, active-duty service members have access to TA money, and honorably discharged veterans have access to their GI Bills. Loans have to be repaid with interest, and you should think carefully before accepting them.

The much-discussed federal Pell Grant is the target for most. Pell Grant money does not need to be paid back. The award must be used for education-related expenses, and only undergraduate students who do not already possess a bachelor's degree are eligible. The maximum award amount for the 2014–2015 academic year is $5,730.

Not everyone rates Pell Grant money. The award is based on financial need, cost of school, and rate of educational pursuit. The Pell Grant award amount can change yearly, and the FAFSA must be reapplied for every academic year. The application will repopulate all of your personal information to help expedite the process.

If a student is awarded Pell Grant money, the amount is sent to the school, and the school pays the student. Federal Pell Grant money is paid in at least two disbursements. Most schools pay students at least once per semester.

If any money is owed toward tuition and fees, schools remove that amount from the Pell Grant award prior to turning the remainder of the money over to the student. Award money is typically turned over to students as a check, cash, or a bank deposit. Since most veteran students' tuition is covered by the GI Bill, most veterans should get to keep the full amount of the award. Remember this prior to choosing an institution that may not be fully covered under Post 9/11 or MGIB.

In order to be eligible to apply for Federal Student Aid, borrowers must meet the following parameters:

- Most programs require demonstrating financial need.
- Must be a U.S. citizen or eligible noncitizen.
- Have a valid Social Security number (exceptions apply).
- Be registered with the Selective Service.
- Be enrolled or accepted at a minimum of half-time as a regular student into an eligible degree or certificate program.
- Maintain satisfactory progress.

Federal Student Aid applicants will also need to sign statements stating:

- Student is not defaulting on any federal student loans.
- Student does not owe money on any federal grants.
- Student will only use aid money for educational-related expenses.

- Student must demonstrate evidence of eligibility by having a high school diploma, GED, or completed home school program approved by state law.

Be sure to research and understand where a student loan is coming from prior to accepting any money. Student loans can be federal or private depending on the source. Federally backed loans and private loans have many differences. Here are just a few of the reasons that federally backed loans can offer greater flexibility than loans from private sources.

- Federal loans can offer borrowers fixed interest rates that are typically lower than private sources of loans.
- Borrowers are given a six-month grace period upon completion of the degree to begin repayments. Often, private school loans will require payments to be made while the student is still attending school.
- Only federally backed loans are subsidized, meaning the government pays the interest for a period of time.
- Interest may be deductible; this is not an option for private loans.
- Federal loans can be consolidated into a Direct Consolidation Loan; private loans cannot.
- Private loans might demand that the individual borrowing the money already has a credit record, but most federal student loans will not perform a credit check.
- Federal loans offer more options for forbearance or deferment.

Federal student loans come in three shapes and sizes. Federal student loans can be Direct Subsidized Loans or Direct Unsubsidized Loans, Direct PLUS Loans (for advanced education), or Federal Perkins Loans.

According to the U.S. Department of Education, Direct Subsidized Loans have slightly better parameters for students with financial need. Direct Subsidized Loans are only available for undergraduate students, and the amount awarded cannot exceed the financial need. Interest on this type of loan is covered by the U.S. Department of Education while students remain in school at a minimum of half-time and for the first six months after graduation (the grace period).

Direct Unsubsidized Loans demand a demonstration of financial need and are available for undergraduate and graduate school. The amount borrowed is regulated by the school and is based upon the school's costs. Interest is the responsibility of the borrower at all times. If the borrower chooses not to pay interest while in school, the amount accrues and is added into the overall loan and will be reflected in payments when they come due.

Federal PLUS loans are available for graduate or professional degree-seeking students and parents of dependent undergraduate students. Schools must participate in the program for students to be eligible. Loans are fixed at 7.9 percent, and borrowers must not have an adverse credit history. PLUS loans do not require financial need and have payback options in case the student has needs above his or her available benefit levels and parents who will help. For more specific information regarding the types of loans available, take a look at the U.S. Department of Education's Federal Student Aid website (http://studentaid.ed.gov/types/loans/federal-vs-private).

If you plan on applying for Federal Student Aid, you will need access to your taxes from the previous year. For example, if you are applying for student aid for the 2014–2015 school year, you will need your 2013 taxes. The FAFSA application opens in January of each year and must be reapplied for each year. Check with your state for possible state-based financial awards and potential deadline dates. For example, California has the CalGrant award. The award is applied for while completing the FAFSA; however, the deadline is set on March 2 of each year. If you are eligible and do not fill out the FAFSA and submit required documents prior to this point, you will not be eligible for any state-based assistance if attending a school in California.

If you do not rate any money one year, do not let it deter you from applying in subsequent years. You may rate it at another time because finances can change. If you are under the age of twenty-four but have already served on active duty (or are currently serving!), you will not need to enter your parents' tax information on the FAFSA (Higher Education Reconciliation Act of 2005). You will enter your personal tax information (most Marine Corps bases have a free tax service available for service members, Volunteer Income Tax Assistance [VITA]).

If you are interested in applying for Federal Student Aid but are unsure how to proceed, contact the Financial Aid office of your school for further guidance.

Here is a quick checklist for applying for federal financial aid:

1. Have your tax information from the previous year on hand.
2. Apply on http://www.pin.ed.gov for your PIN.
3. Apply for Federal Student Aid through FAFSA (http://www.fafsa.ed. gov; you will need to list your school).

4. Verify your submission with your school's Financial Aid Office.
5. Keep an eye out for your financial aid award letter, and monitor your student account on your school's website.
6. Hopefully receive a payment!
7. The http://www.fafsa.ed.gov website offers many helpful hints if you get stuck while filling out the FAFSA. The application will take twenty to thirty minutes to complete online.

GI Bill Top-Up

If a Marine is attending school while on active duty and chooses a school that costs more than the amount allotted under TA, GI Bill Top Up can be used to top off the TA. The Marine would activate his or her GI Bill and tap into it as a funding resource for the portion of the class that was not covered by TA. This would affect the Marine's overall remaining benefit amount upon separation from the military.

TA covers only up to $250 per credit hour. If a Marine chooses a school that costs $350 per semester hour and is taking a three-semester hour class, he or she will be $300 out of pocket after using TA. The remaining amount of money will be his or her responsibility to pay. In this case, Top Up could be used to cover the amount.

Using Top Up may be necessary in some cases, but generally I would avoid the recommendation. Tapping into Top Up will pull on the Marine's available GI Bill months, thereby reducing the amount of benefits remaining after separation from the military.

Many institutions across the country cost less than or equal to the amount covered under TA. If the institution you are planning on attending is over the $250 threshold and recommending GI Bill Top Up, please speak to an academic counselor for advice prior to making any final decisions.

Three situations come to mind when I may discuss using Top Up for service members.

1. If the individual is about to run out of TA money, is at the end of his or her degree, and is separating from active duty soon. In this case, it is important to note that the individual will obtain the degree prior to separating and will be able to list the accomplishment on his or her résumé. This enables the veteran to get into the workforce faster.
2. In most master's degree programs, the cost is above and beyond the $250 per credit hour that TA can cover. Completing an advanced

degree while still on active duty will be an enormous benefit to separating service members.

3. If the service member is looking to attend a prestigious university and cannot cover the costs out of pocket. In this case, I would typically recommend attending a local community college (many have fully online, fast-paced programs available) for as long as possible prior to transferring into the university. At least this way, the individual would not be drawing from his or her GI Bill for such an extended period of time.

For the undergraduate rate of study, try all possibilities prior to looking into Top Up. Oftentimes, the Pell Grant is a viable option (check the "Federal Student Aid" section). Ultimately, the decision to use Top Up must be the service member's, but the guidelines above are solid and should be considered prior to making a move.

SCHOLARSHIPS

For some reason, Marines are loath to apply for scholarships, but military dependents are always ready and prepared to write. Last year, I helped the dependent daughter of a gunnery sergeant friend with several essays for submission to scholarships. She was awarded close to $15,000 for her first year of college! That was a large pot of easy money to help with school. Sound good? If so, read on.

While there is quite a bit of scholarship money available for veterans, you must be proactive in your pursuit. No one is going to hand over the money without you making an effort. Applying for scholarships is not as difficult as it seems. You can often reuse information, so keep everything you write. Most education centers have financial aid packets available for you to pick up or posted on their websites (e.g., Camp Pendleton: http://mccscp.com/jec). These packets offer a good place from which to start your search.

Try to remember that the active-duty TA money only goes so far. TA does not cover books, tools, computers, and so on. Veterans should run the numbers before you start. For example, California State University, Long Beach (CSULB), estimated out the 2013–2014 school year book costs at $1,788. Currently, if a veteran is attending school full-time, the maximum book stipend awarded under the Post 9/11 GI Bill is $1,000 per academic year. That leaves a gap of $788 for the veteran attending CSULB to cover out of pocket. In either case, applying for scholarships is a wise move, although not your only option.

Scholarships come in all shapes and sizes. You will need to determine which scholarships may potentially apply to you. Do not narrow yourself into only veteran-based possibilities. You can apply for civilian scholarships as well. Most break down into specific categories, such as pursuit of study, age, gender, race, disability, state based, or school based.

When you begin your search, remember it will take some time to find and determine eligibility. Start by making a quick search on your school's website. Many schools list scholarships specific to their institution right on their own pages. Check with your school's veterans' representatives, the financial aid department, and the local Education Center for possible scholarship opportunities. Libraries are often another underused resource for scholarship opportunities. Check opportunities based on options outside your military experience. Then check opportunities based on options within the military community. Prepare the best essay possible, and check to see if someone in the Education Center is willing to proofread it for you. Always start far, far in advance. Most scholarships are due during the spring semester timeframe in order to pay out for the following fall.

Be very careful of organizations demanding you pay money in order to be eligible for a scholarship. Scholarship information is widely available, and you should not have to pay to find, receive, or complete an application. Most certainly, *never* give any credit card information. If you need help, contact your school's financial aid department for more guidance.

Military Service–Related Scholarships

The following are just a few of the scholarships available to service members. Take a look and see what might be relevant to you. At the end of the section there are several scholarship search sites listed.

Pat Tillman Scholarship
http://www.pattillmanfoundation.org/tillman-military-scholars/apply/
(480) 621-4074
info@pattillmanfoundation.org
Award amount varies every year. This year's awards per scholar averaged $11,000. That would be money above and beyond your GI Bill. Active-duty, veterans, and spouses of both categories are eligible to apply. Applicant must be attending school full-time at a four-year university or college (public or

private) at the undergraduate or graduate level. This scholarship is a great opportunity for graduate school students, because options at that level are more difficult to find. Applicant must apply for Federal Financial Aid (FAF-SA). Digital files of the applicant's DD-214 or personal service record and résumé will be required in order to submit, as well as responding to the two essay prompts. Those who proceed further will need to turn in their financial aid award letter (from attending institution), SAR report from FAFSA, and a photo highlighting the applicable individual's military service. Application opens in January and closes the following month. Check the website for more information.

American Veterans (AMVETS)
http://www.amvets.org/pdfs/programs_pdfs/scholarship_application_veteran.pdf
(877) 726-8387
Award amount is $4,000 over four years. Applicant must be pursuing full-time study at the undergraduate, graduate, or certification level from an accredited institution. Three scholarships awarded annually. Application is due by April 15. Applicant must be a veteran, be a U.S. citizen, and have financial need. Required materials include the veteran's DD-214, official school transcripts, a completed (and signed) 1040 form, a completed FAFSA application, a 50–100-word essay addressing a specific prompt (see website), a résumé (see website), and proof of school-based expenses.

American Veterans (AMVETS) National Ladies Auxiliary
http://amvetsaux.org/assets/national-scholarship-application.pdf
(301) 459-6255
Two scholarships at $1,000 and up to five scholarships at $750 may be available. In order to be eligible, applicant must be a current member of the AMVETS Ladies Auxiliary, or a son or daughter, stepchild, grandchild, or stepgrandchild of a member. Application can be filled out starting in the eligible individual's second year of undergraduate study at an eligible institution. Required documents include a personal essay of 200–500 words (see website for more information), three letters of recommendation, official transcripts, a copy of the member's membership card, and all required paperwork from the Ladies Auxiliary. Applications are due by July 1.

Military Order of the Purple Heart (MOPH)
www.purpleheart.org/scholarships/Default.aspx
www.purpleheart.org/Downloads/Forms/ScholarshipApplication.pdf
(703) 642-5360
scholarship@purpleheart.org
Be aware that this scholarship demands a $15 payment at time of submittal. Applicant must be a Purple Heart recipient and a member of the Military Order of the Purple Heart, or the spouse, widow, child (step and adopted), or grandchild. Student must currently be a high school senior or attending college as an undergraduate student full-time (or attending trade school), and have a minimum 2.75 GPA on a 4.0 scale. Applicant must submit a 200- to 300-word essay (see site for prompt), two letters of recommendation, all other required materials, and the $15 fee (check or money order).

American Legion Auxiliary
www.alaforveterans.org/Scholarships/Non-Traditional-Student-Scholarship/
Approximately five scholarships at $2,000 are awarded to applicants who are members of the American Legion, American Legion Auxiliary, or Sons of the American Legion. Members must have paid dues for a minimum of two years prior to applying. Applicants must be nontraditional students (going back to school after an absence or starting later in life). Applications are due by March 1.

Marine Memorial Association Scholarship
http://mmanetcom.marineclub.com/ScholarshipsHome
(415) 673-6672
For the current year, the Marine Memorial Scholarship awarded twenty scholarships, two for $10,000, six for $5,000; all other awards are set at $2,500. The scholarship information is posted in January and due in April. Applicants must be active members of the Marine Memorial Association, or dependents or grandchildren of an active member.

Veterans of Foreign Wars (VFW)
http://www.vfw.org/resources/pdf/militaryscholarship.pdf
(816) 756-3390, ext. 220
Twenty-five annual scholarships for VFW members who served or are currently serving in one of the branches, or members of their immediate family. Five scholarships per branch will be awarded at $3,000 apiece. If already

separated, the EAS date must have been within thirty-six months before the December 31 annual deadline.

Armed Forces Communications and Electronics Association (AFCEA)
http://www.afcea.org/education/scholarships/undergraduate/military.asp
(703) 631-6100
Three scholarships are available to eligible veterans through the AFCEA: the Military Personnel/Dependents Scholarship, the Afghanistan and Iraq War Veterans Scholarship, and the Disabled War Veterans Scholarship (Afghanistan or Iraq).

The Military Personnel/Dependents Scholarship awards $2,000. Active-duty service members, veterans, dependents, and spouses may apply, but they must be attending a four-year institution (no community college) full-time. Active-duty military and veterans can apply in their first year of school; however, spouses and dependents must be in their second year at minimum.

AFCEA scholarships require certain fields of study, such as electrical, chemical, systems or aerospace engineering, mathematics, physics, science or mathematics education, technology management, management information systems, or computer science. Majors of study that support U.S. intelligence initiatives or national security may be eligible as well, if the subjects are applicable to the purpose of AFCEA.

Transcripts and two letters of recommendation from faculty members are mandatory.

Disabled American Veterans (DAV) Auxiliary
http://auxiliary.dav.org/membership/Programs.aspx
(877) 426-2838, ext. 4020
Life members with the DAV Auxiliary who are attending a college or vocational school full-time can participate in the scholarship program. The scholarship maxes out at $1,500. Part-time pursuit of study may be eligible for $750. Applicants must maintain a minimum of 12 credit hours per semester to remain eligible. Renewals are not guaranteed.

Society of Sponsors of the United States Navy Centennial Scholarship
http://www.nmcrs.org/education.html, http://www.nmcrs.org/sponsors.pdf
Applicant must be combat-wounded Iraq or Afghanistan veteran (or spouse) with an associate degree (or equivalent credits), pursuing a bachelor's degree (full-time) leading to a teacher credential. Five $3,000 scholarships will be

awarded annually. Applications can be submitted throughout the academic year (August–May) for open enrollment.

Navy and Marine Corps Relief Society
http://www.nmcrs.org/pages/education-loans-and-scholarships
Navy and Marine Corps wounded veterans of OIF, OEF, or Operation New Dawn, or those wounded in operational deployments, major training exercises, or operational mishaps, may be eligible for $3,000 scholarships. Applicants must be pursuing a degree in a teaching profession. Spouses of Wounded Warriors may be eligible as well (teaching profession, medical, or medical-related fields only).

MECEP or MECP Programs-LOAN
http://www.nmcrs.org/pages/education-loans-and-scholarships
Active-duty Marines and sailors accepted into the Marine Enlisted to Commissioning Program (MECEP) or Medical Enlisted Commissioning Program (MECP) may be eligible to apply for a $500–$3,000 loan per year through NMCRS. The interest-free loan must be paid back within forty-eight months of commissioning.

School-Based Scholarships

Many schools offer internal scholarships. Speak to the financial aid department of your chosen institution to find out about potential opportunities. This section demonstrates just a few of the scholarships available around the country.

Florida

Santa Fe College
Jeffrey Mattison Wershow Memorial Scholarship
http://m.sfcollege.edu/development/index.php?section=info/JeffreyMattison
WershowMemorial
Applicant must have received an honorable discharge (but can still be on active duty) and must maintain a minimum of a 2.5 GPA for award renewal. Award amount is $1,600 per year, or $800 per semester. Application demands a 1,000-word essay pertaining to student's education (see website) and three letters of recommendation (see website).

Idaho

Idaho State University
Iwo Jima Scholarship
http://www.isu.edu/scholar/forms/IwoJimaAnn.pdf
The Iwo Jima Scholarship may be available to descendent of World War II veterans (preference for those who served at Iwo Jima). Applicant must have a 3.0 GPA to be eligible and preference is given to engineering majors. Personal statement and discharge papers are required (see website).

Kansas

Johnston County Community College
Veterans Scholarship
http://www.jccc.edu/financialaid/scholarships/institutional-scholarships/veterans/avetrn.html
This scholarship is designed to assist veterans who are re-entering the workforce or higher education after being discharged from active duty or deployment. Funding is available to veterans who have been discharged within six months of the first day of classes of the semester they plan to enroll at JCCC. The scholarship will be applied to tuition and book costs, with no cash going directly to the student. Books must be purchased at the JCCC bookstore.

Dixon Memorial Veterans Scholarship
http://www.jccc.edu/financialaid/scholarships/institutional-scholarships/veterans/fdixvt.html
(913) 469-3840
Veteran applying for scholarship must have completed a minimum of nine credit hours prior to submitting application. Applicant must demonstrate need and have a 2.5 GPA or higher. Student must be enrolled in a minimum of nine credit hours to receive the $500 award and must have submitted all required documents (see website), including a FAFSA application.

Maryland

Wor-Wic Community College
Salisbury Optimist Scholarship
http://www.worwic.edu/StudentServices/FinancialAidScholarships/LocalNeedBasedScholarships.aspx

Applicant must be a resident of Wicomico County, Maryland; must enroll at the college within two years of returning from the military; and must demonstrate financial need. A GPA of 3.0 is necessary to apply.

Michigan

Michigan State University
MSU Disabled Veteran's Assistance Program
http://finaid.msu.edu/veterans.asp
New and returning undergraduate veterans with a military-related disability who are Michigan residents and working on their first baccalaureate degree can potentially qualify for an aid package that covers all costs.

Minnesota

University of Minnesota Duluth
LaVerne Noyes Scholarship
http://www.d.umn.edu/onestop/student-finances/financial-aid/types/
scholarships/umd-current.html
This scholarship is available to students attending the University of Minnesota Duluth. Applicant must be a direct blood descendant of a military member who served in the U.S. Army or Navy in World War I and died in service or received an honorable discharge. Applicant must demonstrate financial need. The award is $1,000.

New York

Cornell University Law School, Dickson Randolph Knott Memorial
http://www.lawschool.cornell.edu/alumni/giving/endowed_funds/
scholarships_g-l.cfm
Applicant must be a military veteran enrolled in the law school (see website for more information).

Monroe Community College
Donald W. Holleder Endowed Scholarship
http://www.monroecc.edu/depts/finaid/documents/
scholarshipbrochurelisting2012_2013.pdf
Applicant must demonstrate financial need, and preference is given to Vietnam veterans and their dependents. The award is for $600 per year.

Ithaca College
The Pervi Family Endowed Scholarship
https://www.ithaca.edu/giving/scholarships/named/hs/
Scholarship preference is given to a Marine who has been wounded in combat and received the Purple Heart, or to the minor dependent of a Marine killed in action. Awarded to a student in the School of Humanities and Sciences with demonstrated financial need.

Hilbert College
Sgt. Martin F. Bogdanowicz Memorial Scholarship
http://www.hilbert.edu/admissions/student-aid/scholarships-grants
Scholarship is for entering freshman veterans (or their children).

Ohio

Cedarville University
James Cain Special Education Award
http://www.cedarville.edu/courses/catalog/2011-2012/financial-information.pdf
Full-time sophomore, junior, or senior students at the university majoring in special education (intent on teaching kids with special needs) may apply. Applicant must demonstrate financial need, and preference is given to certain populations, including those who have served in the military.

Texas

Angelina College
Disabled American Veterans Scholarship
http://www.angelina.edu/financialaid/scholarship.html
Applicant must be a descendent of a member of the DAV. The award is $500 per semester for full-time study.

Texas Christian University
Adrienne Miller Perner Scholarship
http://www.fam.tcu.edu/schol_other.asp
(817) 257-7615
Amount varies. Applicant must be a child or grandchild of a career military service member. Applicant must also be female and majoring in ballet. Scholarship is based on talent or community work.

Utah

Westminster College
Doris Edwards Miller Endowed Scholarship
www.westminstercollege.edu/pdf/financial_aid_current/0910schlplist.pdf
This scholarship is available to veterans or their children, but both must demonstrate need. Full-time enrollment is mandatory in order to be eligible for this scholarship (eight at $3,500).

Scholarship Possibilities for Dependents

Below is a list of scholarships available for spouses and dependent children. Always check with the Officers' Wives Club (OWC) aboard the base where you are stationed if you are still on active duty with the Marine Corps. The OWCs usually have scholarship possibilities every year. Here are the websites to a few of the bases:

- Camp Pendleton: http://www.cpowc.org/
- Camp Lejeune: http://camplejeuneosc.weebly.com/
- MCAS Miramar: http://miramarowc.org/
- Parris Island: http://parrisislandosc.com/
- Quantico: http://www.qoso.org/
- MCAS Yuma: http://yumaosc.blogspot.com/
- Cherry Point: http://cherrypointosc.org/
- Twentynine Palms: http://osc29palms.weebly.com/

Ladies Auxiliary VFW
Continuing Education Scholarship
https://www.ladiesauxvfw.org/images/stories/CONTINUING%20
EDUCATION%20SCHOLARSHIP%20APPLICATION%2013-14.pdf
Spouses, sons, and daughters of members may be eligible if they are pursuing a college degree or a career pathway at a technical school.

Fisher House
http://www.militaryscholar.org/
Scholarships for Military Children Program
http://militaryscholar.org/sfmc/index.html

Run by the commissaries. A minimum of one $2,000 scholarship through every commissary location is awarded, although more might be possible depending on funding. The award may be used for payment of tuition, books, lab fees, or other education-related expenses. Scholarship is open to children of active-duty, retired, or reserve service members. Applicant must have a minimum of a 3.0 GPA on a 4.0 scale.

The Joanne Holbrook Patton Military Spouse Scholarships
http://www.militaryfamily.org/our-programs/military-spouse-scholarships/joanne-holbrook-patton.html
For spouses of active-duty, retired, and reserve service members. This award may be used for tuition, fees, or school room and board. The scholarship offers assistance for GED or ESL, vocational training or certification, under-graduate or graduate degrees, licensure fees, and clinical hours for mental health licensure. Applicants can attend face-to-face schooling or online.

American Legion

http://www.legion.org/scholarships

Samsung American Legion Scholarship
http://www.legion.org/scholarships/215471/download-samsung-scholarship-application
Applicants must have completed a Boys State or Girls State program, be direct descendants or legally adopted children of wartime veterans (must be eligible for American Legion membership), and be in their junior year of high school. The award is up to $20,000 for an undergraduate course of study. Winners are selected based upon academic record, financial need, and participation in community activities. The application requires several mini-essays. Scholarship is for undergraduate study only and is based on financial need. It can be used for tuition, books, fees, or room and board.

Legacy Scholarship
http://www.legion.org/scholarships/legacy
Eligible applicants are children or adopted children of military members who died while on active duty on or after September 11, 2001; are high school seniors or already graduated; and are pursuing an undergraduate degree.

The Baseball Scholarship
http://www.legion.org/scholarships/baseball
baseball@legion.org
Applicant must have graduated high school, be on a team affiliated with an American Legion post, and be on a 2013 roster filed with the National Headquarters. High school transcripts, three letters of testimony, and a completed application must be filed.

National High School Oratorical Contest Scholarship
http://www.legion.org/scholarships/oratorical
oratorical@legion.org
Scholarship money (up to $18,000 for first place) can be used at any college or university within the United States. Scholarship has hundreds of small rewards involved at local levels.

Navy and Marine Corps Relief Society
http://www.nmcrs.org/education.html
Children and spouses of active or retired military may be eligible to apply for interest-free loans and scholarships that range from $500 to $2,500. Applicant must be pursuing full-time study and demonstrate financial need. Loans must be paid back within twenty-four months. Scholarships are only available to spouses and children of service members who died on active duty or in retirement.

Department of Michigan–American Legion Auxiliary
http://michalaux.org/
Michigan Medical Career Scholarship
http://michalaux.org/wp-content/uploads/2013/10/2014-Michigan-Past-President-Parley-Medical-Scholarship-Application.pdf
Applicants should be daughters, granddaughters, great-granddaughters, sons, grandsons, or great-grandsons of honorably discharged or deceased veterans of specific conflicts (World War I, World War II, Korea, Vietnam, Persian Gulf, etc.) and be living in Michigan. The award is $500 for tuition, room and board fees, books, and so on. Scholarship must be used at a school in Michigan, and applicants must be in their senior year of high school (top quarter of their class) and preparing to enter college. This is a need-based scholarship.

Michigan Non-Traditional Scholarship

http://michalaux.org/wp-content/uploads/2013/10/2014-Michigan-Non-Traditional-Scholarship-Application.pdf

One two-year scholarship will be awarded in the amount of $500 per year. Applicant must be the descendent of a veteran, over the age of twenty-two, and attending college or trade school for the first time or attending college after a significantly long break. The award may be used toward tuition and books at a school in the state of Michigan. Entries are due by March 15. Application includes short essays.

National American Legion Auxiliary

Children of Warriors National Presidents' Scholarship

https://www.alaforveterans.org/Scholarships/Children-of-Warriors-National-Presidents--Scholarship/

Fifteen scholarships were awarded in 2012–2013. Applicants must be daughters or sons, stepdaughters or stepsons, grandsons or granddaughters, stepgrandsons or granddaughters, or step-great-grandsons or granddaughters to eligible American Legion members. Applicants should be in their senior year of high school and complete fifty hours of volunteer service. Completed applications and all documentation (includes an essay) are due to the local American Legion Auxiliary Unit by March 1, and winners are announced on March 15.

Spirit of Youth Scholarship

https://www.alaforveterans.org/Scholarships/Spirit-of-Youth-Scholarship-Fund/

Five awards at $5,000 for this scholarship. Applicants must be seniors in high school and junior members of the American Legion Auxiliary for the past three years, hold current membership, and continue membership throughout awarding years. A 3.0 GPA is mandatory for individuals applying for this scholarship. Applications are due by March 1; winners are announced March 15. ACT or SAT scores, high school transcripts, four letters of recommendation, a completed FAFSA application, and essays are required.

Marine Corps Scholarship Foundation

http://www.mcsf.org/eligibility

(703) 549-0060

Applicants must be the son or daughter of one of the following:

- Active-duty or reserve U.S. Marine
- Veteran U.S. Marine who has received an honorable discharge or medical discharge, was wounded, or was killed while serving in the U.S. Marine Corps
- Active-duty or reserve U.S. Navy corpsman who is serving or has served with a U.S. Marine unit
- Veteran U.S. Navy corpsman who has served with a U.S. Marine unit and has received an honorable discharge or medical discharge, was wounded, or was killed in the U.S. Navy

Applicants must meet the following eligibility criteria:

- Planning to attend an accredited undergraduate college or vocational or technical institution in the upcoming academic year, and pursuing a first bachelor's degree or technical certificate. Students attending Federal Service Academies or pursuing graduate degrees are not eligible.
- Family AGI for the 2012 tax year does not exceed $91,000. Nontaxable allowances are not included in determining AGI.
- GPA of at least 2.0 (on a 4.0 scale).

Heroes Tribute Scholarship Program for Children of the Fallen
http://www.mcsf.org/mcsf-content-pages/landing-pages/heroes-tribute-for-the-fallen-program
The Scholarship Foundation guarantees scholarships of up to $30,000 over four years ($7,500 a year) to the following:

- Children of Marines and veteran Marines who were killed in the terrorist attacks on September 11, 2001
- Children of Marines and children of Navy corpsmen attached to a Marine unit, who were killed in combat after September 11, 2001
- Children of Navy Religious Program Specialists attached to a Marine unit, who were killed in combat on or after September 27, 2008
- Children of Marines who were killed in training after September 27, 2008

Heroes Tribute Scholarship Program for Children of the Fallen applicants must meet the established eligibility criteria, excluding the income eligibility requirement.

Limited grandchildren eligibility: The Marine Corps Scholarship Foundation administers scholarship programs of several Marine Corps associations that offer scholarships to the grandchildren of their members. To qualify, a student must provide proof of their grandparent's membership in one of the following associations *AND* meet the established eligibility criteria. There are no exceptions.

- 4th Marine Division Association of World War II
- 5th Marine Division Association of World War II
- 6th Marine Division Association of World War II
- 531 Gray Ghost Squadron Association
- 3rd Battalion/26th Marines
- Basic Class 3-56 Graduate

Other extremely noteworthy options:

The American Military Retirees Scholarships: http://amra1973.org/Scholarship/

The Mike Weston Memorial Scholarship Fund: http://www.pendleton.marines.mil/Portals/98/Docs/SLO/2013%20Weston%20Book%20Scholarship%20description_1.pdf

Federal sites for scholarship searches:

http://www.careerinfonet.org/scholarshipsearch/ScholarshipCategory.asp?searchtype=category&nodeid=22
http://studentaid.ed.gov/

Searches:

https://www.horatioalger.org/scholarships/index.cfm
http://www.collegescholarships.org/scholarships/army.htm
http://www.finaid.org/military/veterans.phtml
http://www.scholarships.com
http://www.collegeboard.org
http://www.scholarships4students.com/council_of_college_and_military_educators_scholarship.htm
http://scholarshipamerica.org/
http://www.careeronestop.org
http://www.collegedata.com
http://www.finaid.org/scholarships/

http://fedmoney.org/
http://www.militaryonesource.com

TEXTBOOK-BUYING OPTIONS

Who knew books could be so expensive? Welcome to college! The cost of books can often get out of control. The Post 9/11 GI Bill maxes out at $1,000 per academic year for books and supplies, and often that does not begin to cover the bill. If you are still on active duty, then you already know that TA does not cover books.

College books are notoriously expensive. Unlike high school, a year of college requires an incredible amount of books. Professors have to find supplemental materials to feed your brain and back up the information with proof. Books are still the most common, easiest way of accomplishing this task.

Now you know why you need them, but not why college books are so expensive. A few reasons come to mind: for example, copyrighted material, specialized material, and online supplements. College books can hold an incredible amount of copyrighted material. Publishers have to cover the copyright fees, as well as all other fees, within the cost of the book. Information within college books is usually quite specialized and often not found elsewhere. This means the books do not have another avenue for sales and contributes to a highly competitive market, driving the cost up. Many books also have online supplements attached to them, and those fees must also be included in the cost.

Last—although I hate addressing this reason, but feel I must—many professors have written books. Can you guess which books could be included in your reading list? Terrible, I agree . . . since professors get royalties just like other authors. Let's think more positively about the situation. Sometimes these books can be some of your most informative and easily organized reference material. Professors often write books based on the knowledge they have derived from their years in the classroom and field experience to help themselves or others teach. Many schools take pride in having such accomplished professors on staff. Speaking from personal experience, getting published is no easy feat. This practice may sometimes help a professor cut down on the book expenses for his or her students because the book follows along closely with the class's learning expectations, thereby allowing the student to purchase one (or at least fewer) books than previously necessary.

Although many other reasons contribute to book costs, I'll get down to the reason you are reading this section: how to pay for them. The first trip to the bookstore can be excruciating as reality sets in. Do not stress yet; other options may exist. Since many books top the $100 range (sometimes closer to $200!), students should spend as much time as feasible trying to find books from alternate sources.

I still recommend checking out the campus bookstore first. Some schools maintain significant used textbook sections. You will need to get to the store as early as possible to take advantage of this possibility; the discounted books will be the first ones to leave the shelves. Check to see if you can sell your books back at the end of the semester as well. Most likely, the amount the store will offer you will be greatly reduced. Try to think of it as "little cash is better than none," and remember that you can roll that money into your textbooks for the following semester.

Next, you can try either renting or buying the books used online. Which path you choose depends on whether you want to keep the books. Personally, because books change every few years and the information within them becomes outdated at such a fast pace, I only kept my French books. The language was not going anywhere, so I figured I would hold on to them for future reference.

There is an astounding number of sites on the Internet that sell or rent used textbooks. Even some bigwigs have gotten into the game. Amazon has a used textbook section that may suit all of your needs. This section (at www. amazon.com/New-Used-Textbooks-Books/b?ie=UTF8&node=465600) permits users to refer friends and earn $5 credits. While it may not seem like much, if you are the first in your group to start referring friends, you could end up with a stash of extra money to help cover your own textbook expenses. Amazon also allows users to sell books back to the store for Amazon gift cards. If you would prefer to rent (yes, for a full semester!), the site has that option available to users. If you are an Amazon Prime member (payment required: join as a student and receive a discount), you can receive your shipment in two days; otherwise, orders over $25 receive free shipping but will run on regular shipment timeframes. Lastly, you can rent or buy Kindle Textbooks for Kindle Fire Tablets, or put the Kindle application on your iPad, Android tablet, PC, or Mac, and read it on your own device. You can rent the eTextbooks for an amount of time you specify. When you pick a book, Amazon lets you set the return date, although the price does go up the longer you keep the book.

Barnes & Noble offers the same services as Amazon (see http://www.
barnesandnoble.com/u/textbooks-college-textbooks/379002366/). You can
receive a check from the store and even get a quick quote by entering some
easy information on the website. The eTextbooks offered through B&N can
be viewed with a seven-day free trial before purchasing on your PC or Mac
(not available for the actual NOOK device or mobile phones). This may
come in handy if you are looking for an older version to save money. Make
sure you compare the older version against a new version (find a friend!)
before purchasing. The eTextbooks are viewed through NOOK Study (free
app). You can highlight, tag, link, and conduct searches on textbooks down-
loaded with this app.

If I were currently attending school, I would ask for gift certificates to
these two stores for every single holiday that came around. The generosity of
family could keep me going with school textbooks for quite some time.

Now, these are not the only two sites to rent or purchase textbooks. Below
are a few other possible sources. Always compare prices at different sites to
make sure you are getting the best deal possible before you proceed.

- Amazon Student Website: www.amazon.com/New-Used-Textbooks-Books/b?ie=UTF8&node=465600
- Barnes & Noble: http://www.barnesandnoble.com/u/textbooks-college-textbooks/379002366/
- Compare book prices:

  http://www.bookfinder4u.com
  http://www.textboorentals.com

- Rent, sell, or buy back books:

  http://www.chegg.com
  http://www.campusbookrentals.com
  http://www.bookrenter.com
  http://www.valorebooks.com
  http://www.skyo.com

Here are my last few ideas on this subject: You may be incredibly
shocked to learn that sometimes the library is a good place to start. Check out
both your college's library and your community library. The book may not
be available for rental for the full semester, but if you only need a section or
two, copy machines will work nicely. Or you can make friends with someone

who already took the class and has not returned his or her book and offer that individual a decent price. Check with the college's bookstore for class reading lists, or send a nice email to the professor to find out the reading list in advance, and then double down on your mission.

Chapter Seven

Prior Learning Credit

Many schools award prior learning credit. Prior learning credit may earn you free college credit and help expedite your degree. Check with the institution you are considering attending to see if they award college credit for military service. If the institution does award credit, they will want to take a look at your official Joint Services Transcript (JST). This may make it possible for you to fast track your college education.

The following topics will be covered within this chapter:

- The American Council on Education (ACE)
- The Joint Service Transcript (JST)
- Subject Matter Proficiency Exams (the College-Level Examination Program [CLEP] and DSST)
- Expeditionary Warfare School and Command and Staff College

THE AMERICAN COUNCIL ON EDUCATION (ACE)

ACE works with the U.S. Department of Defense (DOD) to translate military training and experiences into potential college credit. ACE evaluates Military Occupational Specialties (MOSs), formal courses, and Marine Corps Institute (MCI) classes to determine how they may potentially convert. Once ACE recommends credit for military work, as reflected on the JST, colleges and universities have to determine how to transform those recommendations into academic credit at their particular institutions.

The JST was formerly known as the SMART (Sailor-Marine American Council on Education Transcript). Many readers are probably already aware that the JST exists, but they may still be unfamiliar with the purpose. As outlined in the above paragraph, the JST may potentially help you earn freebie college credit. You read correctly: free credit! That can translate to spending less time in school, graduating earlier, saving GI Bill benefit for a master's degree, or getting into the workforce quicker.

While the process of how ACE translates military work into educational credit is not that exciting, it is important to understand how it occurs in order to comprehend all potential available options while pursuing higher education. Credit recommendations are based on evaluations of military work conducted by college and university faculty members. Chosen faculty must be currently teaching in the specific areas they are in charge of reviewing and understand that learning occurs in nontraditional formats as well as traditional, and preference is given to those who have more than five years of experience. This is a continuous process with new recommendations being added constantly.

More specific information on the translation process can be found on the ACE website (http://www.acenet.edu/news-room/Pages/How-to-use-the-Military-Guide.aspx), but, for the sake of brevity, the faculty reviews the military coursework length, learning outcomes, and instruction and offers credit recommendation. The credit recommendation can be looked upon as a military course description translation to higher education academic coursework. All military courses and MOSs as far back as 1954 have been evaluated. That does not mean that all courses at all times were labeled with credit recommendations.

The ACE website allows users to search for information pertaining to specific military training and schools. Searches can be conducted using military course numbers, military course titles and locations, subject and level, or

ACE identification numbers (the search section of the website is located at http://www.acenet.edu/news-room/Pages/Military-Guide-Online.aspx).

Knowing where to locate information pertaining to military training will make you more informed regarding higher education and potentially able to request work/life credit from your school. Often this type of credit is referred to as nontraditional learning. For example, during my senior year of college I was running short on credits to graduate but was resistant to the idea of returning for another semester (who wouldn't be?). I petitioned my school for permission to prove nontraditional learning experience through a paper. I was given the go-ahead to write a twelve-page paper that demonstrated knowledge earned through work/life experience and how that knowledge related to a particular class the school offered. I am happy to state that I was awarded the credit and managed to graduate at the end of the year!

So, how is this relevant to you? Let's say you decide to attend a school that does not award JST credit. Yes, it is a bummer, but there may still be hope! If you learn how to use the ACE website appropriately, you will have access to descriptions for almost all of your military training. You may be able to petition your school in much the same way I did.

The following is an example of a Marine who is attending George Mason University and is interested in finding more ACE-related information regarding a course he participated in while on active duty to potentially petition his school for credit.

Sergeant Dale attended the Infantry Squad Leader course at Camp Pendleton in May 2010. He would like to see the ACE description of the course to see if it relates to classes and coursework that his university offers. Sergeant Dale gets himself onto the ACE website. He then finds the military "Search Courses" section and inputs the requested information.

The search engine can be tricky to use; I recommend conducting a broad search and reviewing all displayed options. For this example, Sergeant Dale only puts in the course title (Infantry Squad Leader Course), military school or location (Camp Pendleton), and service branch (Marine Corps). Then he reviews the list for the course he wants. Always check the date of course completion to determine which one is relevant.

Sergeant Dale clicks on "Infantry Squad Leader" and is rewarded with a plethora of information. If you are following along with the example, you will see how the information is displayed. The MC code listed (MC-2204-0122) is the ACE identifying number. Searches can also be conducted using these same codes that can be found on the JST.

Sergeant Dale scrolls down to the "Course Number" section. He references his JST transcript (JST is explained in the "Joint Services Transcript (JST)" section of this chapter), where he initially notices the course in the "Other Learning Experiences" section and makes note that the course ID shows M3X, so he knows he completed version 1. Sergeant Dale should determine how long he attended the course, the learning outcomes, the instruction, and a credit recommendation.

Now that Sergeant Dale has access to all of the information pertaining to an infantry squad leader, he can begin comparing it to the classes his school offers. Sergeant Dale finds that George Mason University offers a marksmanship class and decides to petition his school for credit in that subject.

The best recommendation I can give is for Sergeant Dale to write up a brief proposal explaining his participation as infantry squad leader and how that experience directly relates to the marksmanship course offered by the school. Sergeant Dale should include a copy of his military certificate of completion for the course and the ACE description to strengthen his case. Sergeant Dale can also briefly explain why he believes he should be awarded nontraditional learning credit for his active-duty participation in an infantry squad leader's course and submit this proposal to his academic counselor for review and further guidance.

If the school decides to grant Sergeant Dale nontraditional learning credit, it may demand further documentation, possibly a paper. Sergeant Dale may have to further explain how the learning outcomes of the marksmanship course were covered in the infantry squad leader course, what Sergeant Dale took away from his course, and how it is useful in his future life. The decision and requested documentation are entirely up to the academic institution.

JOINT SERVICES TRANSCRIPT (JST)

As mentioned in this chapter, the JST was formerly known as SMART. The Marine Corps, Navy, Coast Guard, and Army are currently participating in the JST.

The JST compiles a Marine's MOS, formal schools, and MCI classes into an academic transcript that can be read and understood by the civilian population in higher education. The JST demonstrates ACE's college credit recommendations for military personnel and endorses a Marine's military experiences as valuable in an academic setting. Schools that award JST credit are essentially offering Marines free elective credit. This can help expedite your college degree and save you money.

The JST is not strictly for academic credit or degree completion. The JST can be used in many different areas, such as employment and skills documentation, state credential verification, and résumé development. If you are putting together a résumé, you can reference your JST for work history. The Transition Assistance Program departments aboard the bases have credentialed résumé writers. This service is free for service members and their dependents. Make sure to bring your JST and Verification of Military Experience and Training (VMET) (https://www.dmdc.osd.mil/tgps/) with you if you schedule an appointment.

According to ACE, "More than 2,300 colleges and universities recognize these transcripts as official documentation of military training and experiences and applicable ACE credit recommendations." That means there is a broad web of schools to choose from that will take a look at your JST and possibly award you some freebie college credits.[1]

Typically, when attending college, students have three different types of credit they must earn: general education, core, and elective. General education credits include math, English, history, arts, health, natural science, and social and behavioral sciences. Core credits include all classes specific to your particular major—for example, business classes if you are a business major. Elective credits are your free choices. They give you a well-rounded education. Your educational pathway will demand a certain number of elective credits depending upon your major course of study. If you chose a major that is heavy on core classes, such as engineering, it will reduce the amount of required elective credits.

JST credit is typically applied to the free-choice elective credits section, although ultimately each school is able to determine what it accepts and how the free credit will be applied. The overall value of a Marine's JST will depend upon his or her chosen MOS, desired educational pathway at an institution that is open to accepting military credit, and completed training. Typically, the longer you are in the military, the more JST you are able to pick up. Remember that since acceptance of the JST is up to the discretion of each institution, some schools will not accept any JST credit. Ahhh . . . the horror! As a counselor, I cannot recommend that you search out schools based on how many free JST credits the institution wants to award you for your military training. In fact, I would be skeptical of an institution that made me big promises. The point in attending school is to get an education, to feed your brain. Choose a school that fits all of your needs, not just the need to finish fast.

I will get into the details of the actual JST in a bit, but first let's discuss how to get it, and what to do with it. For starters, register for an account (at https://jst.doded.mil). Do not use Common Access Card (CAC) access if you are about to separate, since you will no longer have one after your end of active service (EAS) date. Closely follow how the site explains inputting information.

For access to your own JST, go to the "Transcripts" section and print off the "Combo Report." This action will populate the entire JST. From here, you can review your military course completions, military experiences, grades for courses taken with Tuition Assistance money, and any college-level exams (CLEP, SAT, and ACT) you may have taken while on active duty.

You do not need to be on active-duty status in order to access the JST. Nor do you still have to be on active duty to get any mistakes fixed that are found upon review (as discussed in this section). When you print off a "Combo Report," the last page states how you can follow through with corrections. Always double-check the information listed to make sure it is accurate. The copy you print off does not suffice for schools. You must make a request through the website (via the "Transcript Request" tab on the main page) for official transcripts to be sent directly from Pensacola to the institution you plan on attending. If you cannot gain access, contact your local Education Center; they can send the requests as well.

If you are on active duty and notice mistakes in your military training, stop by your local Education Center and request help. If you notice that a particular training is not listed, the Education Centers cannot fix that problem. First, you must run the certificates through the local Installation Personnel Administration Center (IPAC). The Education Center can help you facilitate fixes only for training that already exists on the JST.

Since we are discussing mistakes, I want to skip ahead to discuss the "Other Learning Experiences" section. After pulling your own JST, scroll ahead to this section and review the key. This section basically explains the military work that is not eligible for JST-recommended credit. Why then would I bring it up, you ask? Well, if you see any 4,2 codes together under the "Reason" column for training listed on your JST, you may be losing out on potential freebie college credit. That's right—you have a mistake! These codes may be able to be fixed and the training awarded credit, if credit is recommended. If you are on active duty, dig out your certificate for the listed course and take both the certificate and the JST to your local Education Center. The Education Center can send the information off to Pensacola fairly quickly. If you are not on active duty, follow the guidelines listed on the back page of the JST.

All right, getting back to the start of the JST, let's go through it section by section so you understand how to read it. Therefore, you will be better able to petition your school for elective credit. I promise I will try not to bore you to tears in the process.

- *Military course completions*: detailed explanation of all the courses you completed while on active duty. Each explanation states the credit awarded, if any; how the credit breaks down; and a description of the course. You will notice on the example that marksmanship has been awarded 2SH L. This translates to two semester hours at the lower level (i.e., the freshman and sophomore years of college).
- *Military experience*: includes all of the schools you attended while on active duty. Just like military course completions, detailed descriptions of the courses are followed by credit recommendations, if any.
- *College-level test scores*: any CLEP or DSST exams you have taken aboard the base will show up on the JST in this section. The date, title, recommended amount of credit hours, ACE minimum required score to pass, and score can be viewed.
- *Other learning experiences*: already discussed here.
- *Summary*: this is the best part! Here you can see in an organized fashion exactly what type of credit you possess on your JST. This is the section your counselor will turn to for the academic evaluation. I am going into more detail here, so pay attention! This section rarely looks the same on any two Marines' transcripts. How do you read this section? Well, if you are near a base, go to your closest Education Center and the staff can show you; if not, follow along.

I am looking at Sergeant Dale's Summary section on the JST: Sergeant Dale was a mortarman. He entered the service in 1993. The first training listed is recruit training: October 8, 1993. Below that, the ACE-recommended subject credit is listed as marksmanship, orienteering/outdoor skills, and physical fitness and conditioning.

Scrolling sideways from marksmanship, I can see that two credits at the (lower) level are listed, and the SOC Category Code shows CJ207A. This means that Sergeant Dale has two lower-level credits recommended to him for a criminal justice class. "Lower level" means anything at the freshman-sophomore or community college level. We already understand that his school does not have to award him any credit, but you should also be aware that schools can tweak the ACE recommendations, should they be inclined to do so.

The next course listed is Basic Mortarman, where credit was not recommended. Then we see Personal Financial Management by Correspondence. ACE-recommended subject conversion is Personal Finance, with one credit at the lower level (L) in BU211A/BU211B, or business.

Oftentimes, this section will also have a U or a V. "U" stands for an upper-level credit recommendation. That means anything at the junior or senior level of college. "V" stands for vocational and might be applicable in nontraditional educational environments. Education in a vocational setting typically awards certificates or nondegree diplomas. Sometimes a "G" will be listed, which means ACE is recommending credit at the graduate school level.

The last category is the academic institution courses. First and foremost, this is not an official school transcript. Schools cannot accept this in lieu of official transcripts directly from academic institutions. Here is where you will find a record of all the classes (if any!) that you took while on active duty using Tuition Assistance. Also, your grades will populate if they have been turned in to Pensacola. If you finished a class a while ago and the grade does not appear, contact the Education Center for further guidance. You can get pay checked by Headquarters Marine Corps (HQMC) for unresolved grade issues if they stay on your record for several months.

Looking at the transcript from the viewpoint of an institution, the JST does not have to be converted exactly as shown. JST-recommended credit can be used to knock out a required course, as an optional course that is required within a specific major, as a general elective, to eliminate a prerequisite, or to meet a basic degree requirement. Sometimes further research into a specific ACE-evaluated course could lead to credit above and beyond the ACE recommendation.

Now that the JST is available in digital format, Marines have access to unlimited printed copies from the website. All official transcript requests can be made by the Marine him or herself as opposed to requesting the delivery through the Education Center, but an Education Center official should still review the transcripts for mistakes prior to separation.

The JST can be used for employment as well as education. In this case, the transcript must be requested and delivered in a special manner. See the JST website's "Frequently Asked Questions" section for more information (https://jst.doded.mil/faq.html).

SUBJECT MATTER PROFICIENCY EXAMS

Subject matter proficiency exams allow students to earn college credit by taking exams as opposed to sitting through the traditional class. The exams enable students to save money and time, prepare on their own timeline, and fast track their degrees. All of these reasons are incredibly important for veterans who have to maintain a class load specified by the VA if they want to continue with full benefits.

The Education Centers aboard Marine Corps bases offer the CLEP and DSST. The first exam in every subject is free to active-duty service members. If a service member fails and would like to test again, he or she will need to wait six months and pay a fee (roughly $100 as of mid-2014). Retirees, dependents, and separated Marines can test for the approximately $100 fee as well (be aware that test costs can increase in the future).

The very first thing that students should do prior to taking any CLEP or DSST exams is to verify with their school that the institution accepts these exams and which subjects they accept. No point in taking exams for no reason. Many colleges and universities do accept subject matter proficiency exams, but they limit the amount of credit awarded through this pathway.

After verifying exam acceptance through your school, take a look at www.petersons.com/dod. The Peterson's website maintains free study material for all of the CLEP and DSST exams offered aboard the bases. Now it is time to study, study, study! After all, who wants to pay to test again?

Once you have determined you are ready to test, contact the education center aboard the base and book an appointment. If the local center has computerized testing in place, you will receive instant results for all exams except for the English essay component.

CLEP has thirty-three tests available in five different subject areas: English Composition, Humanities, Mathematics, Natural Science, Social Sciences, and History. The exams cover material typically learned during the first two years of college. The College Composition exam is 120 minutes, but all other exams are ninety minutes. Most exams are multiple choice, although some, including the College Composition, have essays or other varieties of questions. CLEP essays are scored by CLEP or the institution giving the exam. If CLEP holds responsibility for scoring, essays are reviewed and scored by two different English composition professors. The scores are combined and then weighted with the multiple choice section. Exams usually match college classes that are one semester in duration.

The DSST exam program has thirty-eight available tests. DSST exams cover lower- and upper-division classes. This is beneficial for students who have deep knowledge of certain subjects as it will enable them to test further up the degree pathway. Testing further into a specific subject area may also enable a student to participate in classes that can usually only be accessed after prerequisites are completed. Two tests include optional essays, "Ethics in America" and "Technical Writing." Essays are not scored by DSST; they are forwarded to the institution that the test taker designated on his or her application and graded by the college or university. DSST exams are offered only for three-credit courses.

Like I stated earlier, veterans using their GI Bills will benefit greatly by taking and passing CLEP or DSST exams. To maximize the benefit of these exams, tests should be taken (and passed!) while you are still on active duty because that is the timeframe during which you can test for free. Veterans should, however, still consider paying for the exams since the end result can get you into the workforce at a faster pace.

Veterans who take and pass subject matter proficiency exams may potentially reap two major benefits. The first benefit would be created by building a buffer into the required semester credit load. The second benefit would be graduating early.

The VA demands that students maintain a minimum of 12 credit hours per semester in order to rate the full housing and book stipend. Twelve credits equal four classes. Maintaining four classes per semester is not a difficult course load; however, if your goal is a bachelor's degree, and you do not have any previous college credit, five classes (which typically equal fifteen credit hours) will be necessary every semester. Most bachelor's degrees demand 120 credit hours of predetermined courses (found on your degree plan) in order to graduate. Twelve credit hours each semester will total ninety-six credit hours, which are not sufficient to graduate, and you will be out of monthly benefits. If you can add some CLEP or DSST scores into each semester, you will have reduced your required course load.

Reaching graduation early can be a boost to many veterans, especially those with families. Veterans who have completed CLEP or DSST credit may be able to combine those exams with their JST credit and finish their degrees in less than the normally required four years. This enables students to get into the workforce faster or save GI Bill benefit for graduate school, certificate programs, and so on.

ACE also recommends credit for Defense Language Proficiency Tests (DLPTs). The Defense Language Institute Foreign Language Center (DLIFLC) is an actual school that select Marines may attend to become proficient in foreign languages. The DLIFLC produces the DLPTs that the DOD utilizes for military and other select personnel. These exams might be taken while on active duty if you speak a second language. DLPTs score the test takers' reading, listening, and real-life proficiency in a foreign language. In some cases, Marines can receive extra pay on a monthly basis depending upon their scores, the language tested, their current assignment, and possibly the test taker's MOS. If you took a DLPT while on active duty but cannot remember your score, you can check your JST (at https://jst.doded.mil). The ACE policy on DLPT credit can be found online (see http://www.dliflc.edu/academiccreditfo2.html). Ask your school if the institution awards credit for DLPT exams. If you speak a second language and you are still on active duty, contact the local Education Center for more guidance regarding DLPT testing policies. For study materials, visit the DLIFLC website (http://www.dliflc.edu).

Marines with families are always on the lookout for ways to pursue higher education at a faster pace. They are looking for the least amount of interruption to their working careers that is possible while still completing their degrees. This is a reasonable desire since they have families and need to maximize their income-earning potential. Passing CLEP, DSST, or DLPT exams while on active duty can make a major impact on the amount of time these Marines must spend in the classroom at a later date. Often, they study and take several CLEPs on active duty even if they do not elect to take classes until after their separation from the service. Planning for long-term goals and accomplishing what is possible at the moment give Marines good insight into their future academic pathways and help with time management.

EXPEDITIONARY WARFARE SCHOOL AND
COMMAND AND STAFF COLLEGE

Officers (and enlisted personnel) who are Expeditionary Warfare School (EWS) or Command and Staff College (CSC) compliant may be eligible for master's degree credit at a few select schools. University of Oklahoma, University of Maryland University College, Indiana University, Marshall University, Webster University, and Auburn University offer credit for particular pathways of study. The U.S. Marine Corps College of Distance Education and Training (CDET) CSC Distance Education Program has partnered with these schools in order to promote faster academic achievement and success at the graduate level.

To determine which one of these schools will grant prior learning credit for EWS or CSC, visit their website (https://www.tecom.usmc.mil/cdet/sitepages/masters_credit.aspx). Many of the offered options can greatly expedite program completion. Take a look at the different features of each school before making a decision. Here are a few factors you may want to consider:

- Some of the schools offer credit for CSC, but not for EWS
- Cost of attendance for the schools
- Is Tuition Assistance an option for payment, and how much will it cover?
- Is the GI Bill an option for payment, and are you willing to use it?
- Class availability and length
- Area of credit

Officers who are EWS complete can attend Webster or Marshall University as options for expedited graduate degrees. Webster offers more program options, but it costs quite a bit more than Marshall. Students are not limited to these two schools. Other institutions may offer credit for master's programs for EWS or CSC completion. For example, a Marine gunner decided to attend Central Michigan University aboard Camp Pendleton for an MS in administration but was not initially awarded credit for being EWS compliant. He decided to petition the school, and they did grant him credit.

Most of the degrees award credit in the areas of leadership, education, and management. That does not mean you will not be able to receive credit in other areas. CDET has academic Factbooks available with details about each course offered through EWS and CSC. Contact the appropriate individuals by checking https://www.tecom.usmc.mil/cdet/sitepages/contacts.aspx#tab-contacts-OPME to obtain a Factbook for help with petitioning your institution for credit.

Some institutions will take formal submission of your JST as proof of completion for EWS and award credit appropriately. Contact the academic counselor at your school for further advice. Even if you get only one class credited, you will be that much ahead.

Chapter Eight

Standardized Admissions Tests

Whether attending undergraduate or graduate school, oftentimes a standardized admissions test will be required in order to fulfill the admissions application process. Many schools waive this requirement for active-duty service members and veterans. This chapter offers information regarding the following tests, as well as free study materials to help you prepare.

- SAT Reasoning Test (SAT) and ACT
- Graduate Records Exam (GRE) and Graduate Management Admissions Test (GMAT)

SAT AND ACT

http://www.collegeboard.org
http://www.act.org

Depending upon the school you choose to attend, an ACT or SAT score may be necessary for acceptance. Many schools offer veterans flexible admissions by bypassing these exams and taking writing samples and/or placement tests instead. To determine individual requirements, place a call to the veterans' representatives at the school. Typically, a quick call can supply you with all the required application materials.

If the school requires an ACT or SAT score, you need to develop a plan of attack. Application deadline dates, test dates, and study resources need to be located. To find the required application dates, check the school's website and contact the vet reps. In some cases, schools can accept scores at a later date for veterans. Many institutions are aware that oftentimes Marines return from deployment and transition shortly thereafter, leaving little time for test preparation and taking.

Test dates can get tricky. ACT and SAT tests aboard Marine Corps bases are only offered on specific dates, typically once or twice per month. Marines need to book an appointment through their education centers and clear the time with command. Make sure to leave plenty of leeway time to be able to prepare appropriately. SAT and ACT exams should not be taken at a moment's notice if this is avoidable.

Always check with a school to determine which test the institution accepts. Students should focus on that particular test for preparation. Some schools will take either. In that case, students may want to take both and submit their best score.

When testing aboard a base, you can list your school's name or leave it blank. If you decide to take both the SAT and the ACT and submit your top score, do not list the school's name on the test application. If you list the school's name, your scores will go directly to the institution. If you do not list the school's name, you can request that your scores be sent from either organization at a later date. Scores take much longer to come back to the base Education Center than they do to the school or to post on the websites.

If you opt to send your scores to a school or schools during test registration aboard the base (or off-base), you will receive four free score reports for ACT and SAT. If you decide to wait and send your scores after determining the results, each SAT request will cost $11.25 (http://sat.collegeboard.org/

register/us-services-fees#), and each ACT request will cost $12 (http://www. actstudent.org/scores/send/costs.html). If you want to put your best foot forward, my recommendation is to take both tests, wait for your scores to be posted, and then pay to send whichever test produced the most competitive results.

If Marines are not satisfied with their recent score, they may retest the ACT and SAT again off-base during the next test date with no waiting period. On base, a six-month waiting period applies. Marines and sailors receive one test aboard the base for free. Currently, SAT runs $49 and ACT $39 on base.

SAT and ACT scores do not return the next day. Typically, when testing on a base, test scores take approximately ten weeks to be delivered. Scores can be viewed on the SAT and ACT websites earlier, however. ACT multiple-choice scores are typically reported within eight weeks (http://www. actstudent.org/scores/viewing-scores.html), with essay scores reporting roughly two weeks later. SAT scores (http://sat.collegeboard.org/scores/ availability) take approximately three weeks to get posted online.

SAT and ACT are not exactly the same test. Table 8.1 demonstrates some of the differences. For more detailed explanations of the tests, visit the SAT and ACT websites.

You will notice when looking at table 8.1 that SAT does not test science, but ACT does. You will not need to know incredibly specific science information for the ACT; rather, it tests your reading and reasoning skills. SAT has a stronger emphasis on vocabulary, and ACT tests higher-level math concepts than SAT (trigonometry).

The optional essay on ACT is not factored into your composite score. If you take it, the essay is scored separately. The SAT essay is required and factored into the writing score.

ACT keeps each subject area separate, while the SAT subject areas move around, creating a back-and-forth movement. This may be difficult for some test takers.

Remember that free test preparation for both the SAT and the ACT can be found at http://www.petersons.com/dod for military and dependents. Khan Academy (http://www.khanacademy.org) has free test preparation help for the SAT math section. Check YouTube as well for more SAT and ACT videos.

Numerous test preparation companies exist that offer great preparation classes, but there is no reimbursement for this pathway. These programs offer

Table 8.1.

SAT	ACT
Test covers reading, vocabulary, grammar and usage, writing, and math (includes essay)	Test covers grammar and usage, math, reading, science reasoning, and an optional writing section (check with school)
Three main components: critical reasoning, mathematics, and an essay	Five main components: English, mathematics, reading, science, and an optional essay (check if school demands essay)
Test timeframe: 3 hours, 45 minutes	Test timeframe: 3 hours, 30 minutes (4 hours with essay)
Format: multiple choice and grid-in	Format: all multiple choice
Guessing penalty of a quarter-point	No guessing penalty
Measures student's ability to draw inferences, synthesize information, understand the difference between main and supporting ideas, understand vocabulary in context, apply mathematical concepts, problem solve, interpret charts, communicate ideas, revise and edit, and understand grammatical structure	Measures student's written and rhetorical English skills, mathematical skills, reading comprehension, and interpretation, analysis, reasoning, problem solving, and writing skills stressed in high school and entry-level college classes
Scoring: Penalty for guessing; maximum score 2400; each section is worth 800; the average score in 2012 was 1498: critical reading 496, mathematics 514, and writing 488	Scoring: ACT assessment counts only correct answers; composite scores range from 1 to 36, and subscores from 1 to 18; the composite score is an average of the four subscores; the national average in 2012 was 21.1

structured classroom environments and curriculum that may help some service members, but classes do not emphasize an individual's strengths and weaknesses like a self-paced program would allow for. Just remember that "self-paced" means "self-motivated." You have to organize your time and effort on your own.

GRADUATE RECORDS EXAM (GRE) AND GRADUATE MANAGEMENT ADMISSIONS TEST (GMAT)

If you are planning on attending graduate school, you may find that your institution of choice requires a GRE or GMAT score. Just like SAT and ACT, always check with the school to determine which standardized admissions test is required for your graduate school program. Traditionally, the

GRE is taken for most graduate degrees outside of business, and the GMAT is taken for business school. Only the university and college can tell you exactly which test the institution will demand, but taking the GRE might open more options.

Currently, the GRE costs $160 and the GMAT $250. Considering that active-duty service members can receive reimbursement only for one test through DANTES, thorough research might determine which test might be more beneficial. If taking the GRE will enable you to apply to different types of programs and you would like that flexibility, the GRE might be a better option. You can receive reimbursement through your GI Bill, but it will reduce your remaining benefits. If you are still on active duty, it is best to go through DANTES and save all of your education benefits.

In the past few years, the GRE has become more widely accepted for admissions to business schools, and many top-tier universities (such as Yale, Harvard, and Georgetown) have jumped on board. Princeton Review has a link that lists more than seven hundred schools that are currently accepting the GRE for business school (www.princetonreview.com/uploadedFiles/ Sitemap/Home_Page/Business_Hub/Opinions_and_Advice/MBAAccepting GRE.pdf). Try an initial search, then cross-reference with the institutions that interest you. If your institution of choice accepts either, try taking a practice exam for each test first (check both websites). You might find that you have an aptitude for one over the other.

FREE TEST PREPARATION

GRE: www.ets.org/s/gre/pdf/practice_book_GRE_pb_revised_general_ test.pdf

GMAT: http://www.mba.com/the-gmat/download-free-test-preparation- software.aspx

Georgetown University: www.youtube.com/watch?v=xFyqJSucqSo

Others: www.petersons.com/dod, www.khanacademy.org (GMAT math)

Reimbursement

Reimbursement While on Active Duty

To receive reimbursement through DANTES for either the GRE or the GMAT, visit your local education center for the correct forms, or follow these steps:

1. Visit the following links to download the appropriate reimbursement forms:

> GMAT: http://www.dantes.doded.mil/Programs/Exams_GMAT.html
>
> GRE: http://www.dantes.doded.mil/Programs/Exams_GRE.html

2. Sign up and take the GRE or GMAT.
3. Receive official GRE or GMAT scores (about two weeks).
4. Fill out the appropriate forms, and return them to the Education Center's Test Control Officer within ninety days of testing.
5. The applicant is responsible for all testing fees upfront.

Veterans' Reimbursement

Veterans can be reimbursed through the GI Bill. See http://www.gibill.va.gov or call 1-888-GIBILL-1.

Chapter Nine

Free Subject Matter Study Support

This chapter will be short and sweet. I packed it full of free websites and preparatory programs that can help in your educational pursuits. Often, all it takes is a little extra help or a different explanation of the same material in order to clear out the cobwebs and make progress in a subject. I find the websites listed here to have the best information and explanations that can help promote learning. The Military Academic Skills Program (MASP) is included in the military-based reference section. The free course is offered aboard many Marine Corps bases. MASP is an amazing class that may help you begin your educational pursuits in a stronger position.

MILITARY BASED

Peterson's, a Nelnet Company
http://www.petersons.com/dod
Peterson's is incredibly comprehensive. Pretty much anything you need, you will be able to find on this site. You can continue to use this site upon separation from the Corps. Here is a basic rundown of what you and your dependents (free for them as well) can access on the site:

- SAT and ACT prep
- College-Level Examination Program (CLEP) prep (check out the "CLEP" section for more info)
- DSST prep (check out the "CLEP" section for more info)
- Armed Services Vocational Aptitude Battery (ASVAB) prep
- AFOQT Air Force
- Military flight aptitude prep
- GED prep
- GRE and GMAT prep
- LSAT prep
- NCLEX PN/RN (nursing)
- PRAXIS I and II

This site also has options to help users narrow down their searches—for example, by undergraduate and graduate school, vocational-technical school, or Servicemembers Opportunity Colleges (SOCs). The undergraduate and graduate school search tabs have helpful articles listed that may give you more guidance in your pursuit of an appropriate school or an appropriate program, or when you are preparing for the admissions process, which can be very long and time-consuming.

Lastly, on the home page of Peterson's there is a link labeled "OASC" for the Online Academic Skills Course. If you are familiar with MASP, OASC is like an online self-paced MASP class. The program is intended to help boost the user's reading comprehension, vocabulary, and math abilities. The pre-assessment will determine the user's strengths and weaknesses and help design an appropriate learning plan. As a user progresses through OASC, learning is supported by interactive exercises and quizzes.

eKnowledge Corporation and NFL Players
SAT and ACT test preparation
http://www.eknowledge.com/military
(770) 992-0900
LoriCaputo@eknowledge.com
This program is a combined effort of the U.S. Department of Defense and some patriotic NFL players. eKnowledge Corporation donates SAT and ACT test preparation software to military families and veterans. The software usually runs approximately $200 but is free for service members and their families. The programs include classroom instruction, interactive learning participation, and 120 classroom video lessons.

Veterans Attending School with the GI Bill—Tutoring Available
http://www.gibill.va.gov/resources/education_resources/programs/tutorial_
assistance_program.html
Veterans attending school on a Montgomery GI Bill (MGIB) at one-half time or more in a postsecondary program at an educational institution may be eligible for an extra tutoring stipend from the VA. The VA will pay up to $100 per month for tutoring on top of your regular GI Bill payments. The subject must be mandatory for program completion. The total amount cannot exceed $1,200. Student must need help in the subject and, even if currently receiving a passing grade, can receive the assistance if the current grade will not count toward program completion.

Under Post 9/11, there is no entitlement charge (deduction of remaining months of benefit); under MGIB, there is no entitlement charge for the first $600.

Military Academic Skills Program (MASP)
MASP was created as an on-duty educational program that can enhance the English, math, and communication skills of attendees. Although MASP has many benefits, the program is required for Marines who would like to use their Tuition Assistance (TA) money, have General Technical (GT) scores below 100, and do not achieve the required TA qualifying score on the Test of Adult Education (TABE).

The TABE is a remedial math and English exam. It tests reading comprehension, spelling, grammar, and math. The exam is scored through 12.9, which is proficiency through the end of the senior year of high school. TA requires proficiency at the 10.2 level or higher. That equates to the end of the second month of the sophomore year of high school.

Most Marine Corps bases run MASP, but the program operates on a different timeline depending upon the base. Pendleton's MASP runs thirty days, Lejeune hosts day-and-night cohorts that both run six weeks in length, and Miramar's MASP course is a quick two weeks.

MASP is taught by professors who typically instruct at the local area schools. For example, Pendleton's MASP is taught by Palomar Community College instructors, and Miramar's MASP is taught by San Diego Community College District professors. The professors specialize in adult education.

MASP was not designed to boost the Armed Forces Classification Test, ASVAB, SAT, or ACT scores, but the program may inadvertently help. Although the course will typically help increase the GT component of the ASVAB, I would recommend supplementing your studies with http://www.petersons.com/DOD if such is your intent. If you have not taken math or English in a few years and need to take an SAT or ACT, MASP would be beneficial, but check Peterson's and eKnowledge as well.

MASP is remedial and does a great job of preparing separating Marines for a more successful start at school. Since the class typically requires Temporary Additional Duty (TAD) orders from your command, sometimes Marines have a hard time getting permission to attend. If you find yourself in this situation, try the OASC option (at http://www.petersons.com/DOD). OASC is like an online, self-paced MASP.

Did I mention that MASP is free? Spouses, veterans, and civilians are able to attend as well. To attend a MASP session on your base, contact your local education center for information on dates, times, and how to enroll. If your GT score is over 100 but you would still like to attend MASP, you may do so. The TABE is required for anyone who would like to attend MASP, including those who have GT scores above 100, spouses, and civilians. Marines must secure permissive TAD orders through their commands to attend the course.

MASP can also help transitioning Marines prepare for higher education prior to their separation. The course is beneficial in helping Marines start school at a higher base point. Many Marines complain that they feel cobwebs have moved into their brains. Attending this course prior to separating will help clear them out.

MASP is also beneficial for those who need to take an SAT, ACT, or placement exam for their school. Since it is a remedial program, those who attend will get a boost in their test preparation. However, other preparation will need to be pursued for SAT or ACT test takers.

Many Marines opt for MASP prior to retaking the ASVAB. The program might help those who need to boost their GT scores, but I would not rely on it solely. Attending MASP while using supplementary materials geared for ASVAB practice would be a better move.

NON-MILITARY-SUPPORTED FREE SUBJECT MATTER HELP

On to non-military-related helpful study sites. Here is a list of free websites I like to use when I need extra help. I have used all of them at some point and found each one of them beneficial for one thing or another. Hopefully, you will find them constructive too.

Math

Khan Academy
http://www.khanacademy.org
The very first website that should be on anyone's list for math is Khan Academy. This is far and away the most amazing math help available without paying for one-on-one tutoring. You can register for the site through Facebook or Google, and it is incredibly easy to use (and of course FREE!). Videos guide the user through different problems, and discussion question threads allow the user to ask questions. The site offers other subjects besides math. Science and economics, humanities, computer science, and some test prep help are available as well.

Purple Math
http://www.purplemath.com
Purple Math offers a wide array of math topics. You can find anything you might need on the site. The main page is a bit jumbled, and many of the links take you to external sites. Stick to the main Purple Math page. The examples are written out step-by-step to show you how to proceed for each particular problem.

English

Grammar Bytes
http://www.chompchomp.com

I dig this website. The layout is easy to understand and straight-up, meaning there is no mumbo-jumbo to sort through. Each section has a print tab that organizes the material in an easily printed (no pictures or extra garbage to waste ink!), easily read manner. The subject matter is comprehensive, and the site even has some YouTube videos to check out.

Purdue Owl
http://owl.english.purdue.edu/owl/
As an English teacher, I love Purdue Owl. Everything I need is on this site. Plus the site offers instructive writing help, such as thesis statement development, dealing with writer's block, and creating an outline to start a paper. If you are in need of American Psychological Association (APA) or Modern Language Association (MLA) formatting help, this is where to go. APA and MLA are formatting structures that most higher education classes demand be used in paper writing.

Guide to Grammar Writing
http://grammar.ccc.commnet.edu/grammar/
This is a no-nonsense website that has all of the basics organized in a user-friendly manner. The "Editing and Rewriting Skills" section has a checklist that is similar to the one I use when writing and grading papers. The checklist also offers the user links to some of the most common grammatical problems facing writers.

The Grammar Book
http://www.grammarbook.com
Another good no-nonsense English grammar website. The explanations are brief and easy to understand. The examples are to the point and easy to follow. The "Quizzes" tab also has two sections of comprehensive free activities to test your aptitude.

Citation Machine and KnightCite
http://citationmachine.net/index2.php
https://www.calvin.edu/library/knightcite/
These provide citation formatting for APA and MLA references.

APA Format Guidance

American Psychological Association
http://www.apastyle.org

Purdue Owl
https://owl.english.purdue.edu/owl/resource/560/01/

MLA Format Guidance

Cornell University Library
http://www.library.cornell.edu/resrch/citmanage/mla

California State University, Los Angeles
http://web.calstatela.edu/library/guides/3mla.pdf

Purdue Owl
https://owl.english.purdue.edu/owl/resource/747/01/

Veterans Upward Bound (VUB)

http://www.navub.org/

Veterans Upward Bound (VUB) is a U.S. Department of Education program that assists and promotes veteran success within higher education. The free program aids veteran students who have not been to school for a long period of time, or simply need a refresher by assisting in academic preparation. The programs are conducted on college campuses. "The primary goal of the program is to increase the rate at which participants enroll in and complete postsecondary education programs."[1]

Participants in VUB may receive academic skills assessment and refresher courses to enhance their college-level skills. The courses consist of subjects such as math, science, English, computers, and foreign languages. Veteran education services may also be available—for example, assistance completing college admissions applications or GI Bill applications, academic advising, tutoring, or cultural field trips.

Veterans must have the following in order to qualify:

• Have completed a minimum of 180 days of active service, or have been discharged prior to that point because of a service-connected disability *OR*

have been with a reserve component that served on active duty on or after September 11, 2001, for a contingency operation
- Any discharge other than dishonorable
- Must be low income (based upon family income and number of household dependents) *OR* be a first-generation college student (parents do not have degrees)

To find a VUB program in a specific state, check the following link, and contact the program director:

http://www.navub.org/VUB-Program-Information.html

Information about the program can also be found on the Department of Education's website:

http://www2.ed.gov/programs/triovub/index.html

Chapter Ten

Troops to Teachers (TTT)

Troops to Teachers is a U.S. Department of Defense (DOD) program that may help eligible service members pursue a career as a teacher in the public K–12 school system.

The program has two pathways:

1. Counseling pertaining to credentialing pathways and resources to help the service member or veteran achieve success
2. Financial support to help obtain a credential (note that this pathway incurs a three-year payback commitment)

The thought process behind TTT is to empower service members and veterans to pursue secondary careers as public school teachers while filling teacher shortage needs, especially in subjects such as math and science. The program aims to supply schools that maintain populations of low-income families with highly qualified teachers.

While TTT itself does not train veterans to be teachers, the counselors do give guidance and direct eligible personnel toward appropriate credentialing programs. I am a credentialed English teacher and have a few of my own ideas (which I will go into more depth on within this chapter).

At this time, education in this country is taking a beating. There have been massive teacher furloughs and big pay cuts in many states. There are very few areas in this country not facing teacher shortages. This will hopefully change in the future, but there are no guarantees. Take a look at all possible options to protect your future—for example, private schools, community colleges (maybe a different education pathway!), teaching abroad (sounds like fun, right?), online teaching, and charter schools, just to name a few.

Any resource offered should be looked into as a possible information-gathering activity, including TTT. Check with your state's chapter (http://troopstoteachers.net/Portals/1/National%20Home%20Page/stateoffices.pdf) to determine exactly what they can offer you. Almost every state has a chapter. If your state does not, check with the national TTT department at (850) 452-1242 or (800) 231-6242, or via e-mail at ttt@navy.mil.

TTT can be used by eligible personnel while still on active duty; however, you must be within one year of retirement. Also, the program does not participate in job placement, but the website does offer the links to each state's teacher job banks for self-directed searching. If you are a veteran and have already exhausted your GI Bill, TTT may give you the money you need to pursue a teacher credential.

Before you follow through on your decision to be a teacher, read below and check out the TTT website (http://www.dantes.doded.mil/Programs/TTT_GettingStarted.html) for some good advice.

THOUGHTS FOR TEACHER CREDENTIALING

Teacher-credentialing programs are next to impossible to complete while on active duty. They always require some form of student teaching, possibly ranging from six weeks to a full semester of school. If you are on active duty, would like to be a teacher, and do not have a bachelor's degree in an applicable subject, that should be your first goal.

Always contact the state credentialing authority first. You need to determine an appropriate pathway based on the information the state gives you. State governments usually maintain this information on their websites, which can be found with a quick Google search. Second, research the schools in that particular state, and determine the academic pathways they follow to obtain a teaching credential and/or bachelor's degree that leads in that direction. I work with many Marines who attend their community colleges from back home online while on active duty. Check the Department of Defense Memorandum of Understanding website (http://www.dodmou.com) to see if your school is eligible for tuition assistance.

If you are unable to attend a school in your desired state, make an appointment at your local education center to find an available equivalent pathway in your current location, or complete your own search on the College Navigator website.

You can always consider the time you have left while on active duty. Maybe a better pathway for you if you are just getting started would be to attend a local community college and begin working toward the credit you will need in order to finish at a school back home. You cannot go wrong by starting with general education classes: math, English, arts and humanities, social and behavior sciences, and sciences.

If this is the case, contact the four-year university you are interested in attending and obtain a degree plan for the academic pathway they recommend; bring it with you to meet the education counselor. He or she will help you find a college that you can attend while on active duty that will enable you to fulfill the prescribed parameters. Typically, a state community college will provide you with the safest transfer credit. After you find a local school to attend, you will need to contact the future school and ask about transferability of the credits. Many schools have strict transfer guidelines you must abide by.

Many teacher-credentialing programs take more time than just a bachelor's degree, but some do not. Check with the schools in the state where you want to earn a credential to determine the proper pathway. You also might prefer to complete a master's degree with an attached credentialing program. Typically, a master's degree will earn you more money as a teacher. You may get an extra yearly stipend, which may push you up the pay scale because it is college credit above and beyond a bachelor's degree.

Since both GI Bills afford you only thirty-six months of benefit, you may not have enough to finish a full bachelor's degree and credentialing program. So think ahead! Whatever you manage to get done while you are still on active duty is less work you will need to do after you separate. This pathway will save you time, money, and potentially some GI Bill benefit to use toward a master's degree at a later date. Many of the clients I have worked with prefer to finish their bachelor's degree while on active duty (if possible) and then use their GI Bill for a master's degree and/or a credentialing program after separation.

Chapter Eleven

On-the-Job Training and Apprenticeship Programs

- OJT and Apprenticeship Programs
- GI Bill
- United Services Military Apprenticeship Program (USMAP)

OJT AND APPRENTICESHIP PROGRAMS

Oftentimes, Marines are not interested in traditional education and are disappointed that the GI Bill will not be able to help them after they separate. But the GI Bills will cover an array of education types, not just the traditional sort. Learning a trade or a skill while using a GI Bill is possible, and many Marines prefer to pursue an apprenticeship or OJT training program instead of a strictly academic pathway. In fact, many continue down the same pathway they were on while on active duty. The USMAP may also be an available benefit if you are still on active duty.

On-the-Job Training (OJT)

What is OJT, you ask? Well, it is designed to help hire and train employees who do not already possess the required knowledge for the position. The method is commonly used in order to increase productivity and develop an employee's skill base. Training is hands-on, somewhere between six months and two years, and is usually done at the worksite as opposed to a classroom setting for traditional education. Typically, a mentor is assigned to each individual (mandatory for the GI Bills) within the program in order for training to be planned and implemented more effectively. Some potential fields of employment for OJT are heating and air conditioning, law enforcement, welding, electrical work, and auto mechanics. Be aware that OJT is not an apprenticeship program. OJT does not have an instruction portion that requires you to attend classes.

There are numerous benefits to participating in OJT for the employers and for the employee. Employers training employees using OJT promote a good public image through their commitment to the community, help create a more skilled workforce, and see immediate return on their investment since the employee is trained to specific company-driven standards. Employees benefit by earning wages as they learn a new skill, gaining job experience immediately, developing a new marketable skill set, and earning certifications or journeyman standing. Productivity is increased on both sides as training progresses, as does trust as relationships develop through teamwork.

If you were recently hired at a new job, and your employer does not currently participate in OJT programs with the VA, contact the State Approving Agency (http://www.nasaa-vetseducation.com/contacts/default.aspx) to determine if it is possible to facilitate your OJT with the GI Bill. The State Approving Authority within each state approves OJT programs within its borders. If you are looking for a program that is VA approved, contact the same website, or search participating employers (at http://inquiry.vba.va.gov/weamspub/buildSearchInstitutionCriteria.do).

Apprenticeship Programs

Like OJT, the GI Bill can be used toward apprenticeship training. Apprenticeships are programs lasting a specific amount of time while you work under a tradesman before you earn the same status. Apprenticeship programs are common in trades that are skill based, such as welding and electrical work. Oftentimes, skilled trades require formal licensure, which is obtained partly by working under a journeyman within the field.

Apprenticeship programs can last anywhere from one to six years depending upon the technical field. Assessments throughout the program, mandatory testing, and work inspection conducted by a master tradesman are part of the apprenticeship process. Formal classroom training is part of an apprenticeship. Classes typically include general education, such as math and English, and classes pertaining to technical theory and applied skills. State-mandated licensing for many fields, such as plumbing, can demand numerous study hours and formal preparation prior to testing.

Apprenticeship is only just the starting point; journeyman and master tradesman are the following two steps. Apprentices are overseen by a journeyman or master tradesman, and ultimately they are responsible for your work at that time. The goal, over time and with continuing education, is to reach journeyman or master tradesman status. High-level tradesman status leads to higher pay.

The U.S. Department of Labor's (DOL) website has a wealth of information regarding apprenticeship programs (http://www.doleta.gov/oa/). The site explains how registered apprenticeship programs train skilled workers to meet the needs of American industry in fields such as energy and telecommunications. The DOL site has links to search for state apprenticeship agencies, all approved apprenticeship programs, and state-based program sponsors.

Last week, I spoke with a Marine who had separated from the service and was back home in southern Illinois. He was interested in an HVAC program and was wondering if I could help. I found him a contact through an Illinois Department of Veterans Affairs search (located at https://www2.illinois.gov/veterans/benefits/Pages/training-programs-directory.aspx) and explained to him how he was going to use his GI Bill for the training. Contacts can also be found on the National Association of State Approving Agencies website (www.nasaa-vetseducation.com/contacts/default.aspx). This Marine had no idea that he would be able to access GI Bill benefits for an apprenticeship program and was happy he made the call.

Participants in registered apprenticeship programs receive pay starting from the first day of the program, and this pay will grow over time as the apprentice learns more skill. Many programs have mandatory college classes, usually at the local community college, built into the program. Typically, these classes are paid for by the employer. Participants in apprenticeship programs often finish without any education debt. Completing a registered apprenticeship program earns participants certification that is recognized across the country, making them highly portable career fields. According to the DOL, "In the U.S. today, some 37,000 program sponsors, representing over a quarter million employers, industries and companies, offer registered apprenticeship training to approximately 440,000 apprentices. These training programs serve a diverse population which includes minorities, women, youth, and dislocated workers."[1]

Apprenticeship programs are found in a broad range of industries, including construction, manufacturing, public utilities, health care, and the military (read the "USMAP" section). Apprentice-able occupations come in all shapes and sizes, including airfield management, automobile mechanic, welder, and cabinet maker. Major companies such as UPS, CVS, Simplex-Grinnell, Werner Enterprises, and CN (railways) provide apprenticeship opportunities.

Green technology has a bright future for growth. Areas such as recycling in the green technology field have some of the fastest-growing apprenticeship programs. Wind turbine technicians, hydrologists, and toxic waste cleanup specialists are all in demand.

GI BILLS AND TRAINING

Either the Montgomery GI Bill (MGIB) or Post 9/11 may be used for OJT. If you rate both, double-check with the institution you are planning on working within to determine the best pathway, or contact the VA directly (1-888-GIBILL-1).

The Post 9/11 GI Bill pays a scaled monthly housing allowance (MHA) if you are accepted into an eligible OJT or apprenticeship program. You will earn wages from the company training you as well, although normally wages are low while participating in OJT, since both OJT and apprenticeship pay are usually not a percentage of (or related at all to) journeyman pay.

Post 9/11 payments for apprenticeship programs:

- 100 percent of your applicable MHA for the first six months of training
- 80 percent of your applicable MHA for the second six months of training
- 60 percent of your applicable MHA for the third six months of training
- 40 percent of your applicable MHA for the fourth six months of training
- 20 percent of your applicable MHA for the remainder of the training

As your wages increase, the GI Bill payments decrease. A maximum of $83 per month for a book stipend can also be received during training.

Current MGIB payments as of October 1, 2013, are as follows:

- First six months: $1,236.00
- Second six months: $906.40
- Remaining training time: $576.80

The VA maintains rules pertaining to how OJT must be run and whether a program is or can be eligible. For example, the length of the OJT program should be equivalent to what is normally required (for civilians), and the program must encompass the knowledge and skills demanded for the position. Participants should earn equivalent wages to a civilian partaking in the same program, and starting wages should be set with consideration of the previous experience of the participant. All records of the program need to be kept adequately and orderly to verify training with the VA.

Using the GI Bill for OJT purposes is not allowed while on active duty, nor can spouses who have had GI Bill benefits transferred to them participate.

Most states have listings of the available OJT and apprenticeship programs for residents on the state government website. Spend time looking through the DOL section, and take a look at the state VA website. You can also contact your VA Regional Office for help (at http://www2.va.gov/directory/guide/map_flsh.asp). On the National Association of State Approving Agencies (NASAA) website (http://www.nasaa-vetseducation.com/), under the "Programs" tab, you can search approved education and training programs, which include universities, certificate programs, flight school, correspondence school, and OJT-approved programs. You can also access the approved license and certification programs and approved national exams lists.

USMAP

https://usmap.cnet.navy.mil

The United Services Military Apprenticeship Program is an apprenticeship opportunity for active-duty Marines, sailors, and Coast Guard members. The DOL oversees the "Certificate of Completion" for the program, which is nationally recognized. The program enables service members to demonstrate and translate to potential civilian employers, in civilian terms, the skills and knowledge they learned while working in their Military Occupational Specialties (MOSs).

Let's talk about apprenticeships for a minute. Registered apprenticeship programs certify occupational expertise. Apprenticeship completion demonstrates participants' industry-focused skills. Completed programs can help with career advancement and wage increases. The apprenticeship technique has been used in the United States for many decades. Workers who complete apprenticeships are considered more qualified and can demand higher wages. In turn, this enables employers to develop a more productive, qualified staff that has been trained to industry standards.

Getting back to USMAP, I know many of you reading this book are going to be upset when I discuss a few of the requirements. First, you must have enough time on active duty left to be able to complete a certificate. Usually, that is a minimum of one year or maybe more, depending on the requirements for your MOS. Second, there are currently no infantry MOSs available on the program.

Go ahead and complain . . . I'll wait. . . . OK, ready? So, why did I include this in the book when the book is geared to help you transition? Well, some people, believe it or not, start preparing for transition long in advance and may still have enough time to complete a USMAP certificate. Also, I thought about all the other Marines and sailors you may know who have more time left on contract. Other readers may decide to re-enlist. I figured that friends let friends know about good opportunities they find even if the opportunity is not available for them.

To my grunts reading this book, don't hate! My husband (twenty years in the infantry and still going strong!) was outraged when I explained the lack of infantry MOSs. He didn't think it was nice of the DOL to offer the program to almost every MOS besides infantry. After he calmed down, I explained that the program demonstrates the parallels between many active-duty MOSs and equivalent civilian jobs. Unfortunately, badass ninja assassin is a hard one to sell. However, in chapter 12, we will discuss the Army and Navy Credentialing Opportunities On-Line (COOL) websites. The Army COOL "Infantryman" section has a wealth of information for grunts to explore, including applicable civilian-sector certification programs and careers.

Now, if you are still reading, there are two USMAP options for grunts if you are still on active duty and intend to go on Marine Security Guard (MSG) duty or recruiting duty. Both of these options must be started and finished while holding that specific position. The certificate earned for recruiting duty is that of counselor, which is the same certificate that Marines earn in the career planners MOS. The certificate for MSG duty is for security guard. The certificates cannot be backdated for already completing one of these B-billets.

To sign up for USMAP, go to the website listed above, check your eligibility (be on active duty, have a high school diploma or GED, hold an MOS, have enough time in service left), and follow the directions. If you need help, contact your local education center. Many bases have an individual in the department who is qualified to give USMAP briefs. Camp Pendleton Education Center has three counselors with their own USMAP certificates. These gentlemen are more than willing to come to your unit and brief the Marines. You can also set up counseling appointments with these three individuals for help signing up and staying on track with the program. Occasionally, the gentleman in charge of USMAP in Pensacola will even visit a base and brief Marines.

The website is easy to navigate, and many of your questions can be answered in the "Help" section under the "Frequently Asked Questions" tab. To see if you have a certificate available under your MOS, go to https://usmap.cnet.navy.mil, click on "Trades," and then click on "Marine MOS." Many MOSs have more than one certificate available, and some have special requirements as well. Initially, find the one that best suits your daily job; however, if you are eligible, you can try to complete all of them.

Let's take a look at the 2147 MOS of LAV Mechanic. The trade you select must be your primary job. Several different certificates are listed, and all but one require eight thousand hours. Some of the certificate numbers have an N for Navy; some have an M for Marine Corps listed. You can choose either one, depending upon your specific daily occupation (it doesn't matter if you are Navy or Marine Corps; they are interchangeable). Some of these certifications have additional requirements that must be followed. This particular MOS has an additional requirement listed on the right-hand side. The requirement states, "MM (machinist mate) must be E-5 or above and requires both NEC 4231 and 4246," which means that if you were a sailor, you would need to be an E-5 or higher in order to participate in this certificate. If you are a Marine, you are good to go! If your certificate has an additional requirement listed that you do not meet, you can try to petition USMAP directly for permission to proceed.

When checking your MOS requirements, you will also note that each certificate is broken down into sections of required hours. Do not discard the certificate even if your job does not currently include hours within that field. Contact USMAP for further advice at (850) 473-6157 or USMAP@navy.mil if you find yourself stuck and need further assistance.

Now that you know whether you qualify and which certificate you are going to complete, let's discuss how the program works. First of all, it is free and does not require any extra class time! Excited yet? You should be. Basically, the entire program only requires you to log the hours you are already working. USMAP will even backdate a thousand hours for every year you have served in the fleet, up to 50 percent of your required amount!

Here is a hypothetical situation:

Sergeant Jackson has been in the Corps for six years. He is a 2147 and has just signed up for a USMAP certificate. His certificate requires eight thousand hours. USMAP will backdate four thousand hours toward the requirement for his certificate (six years in service, five in the fleet, and a maximum of 50 percent of required hours can be backdated at one thousand per year). He will only need to log the last four thousand, not the original eight thousand. USMAP will backdate hours for each certificate he is eligible to complete. Try to maintain an accurate logbook, because your future employer may ask to see it!

At the end of every week, Sergeant Jackson will get his staff sergeant to sign off on his weekly logs. He will keep a hard copy in a folder if needed for future reference. Twice a year, Sergeant Jackson will get an E-7 or higher or an officer to sign off on his paperwork. Sergeant Jackson will send this semiannual documentation to USMAP in Pensacola. There, they will record his biannual logs. When he attains the four thousand hours needed for the program, Pensacola will send him his certificate. The entire process is incredibly easy as long as you remember to track your hours and consistently send them to Pensacola.

At the end of the program, you will have documented evidence of your work (that civilians can actually understand), including a nationally recognized federal apprenticeship completed and ready to list on your résumé. Even if you do not stay within the same field (MOS) upon separating from the Corps, the certification can still go on your résumé to demonstrate your high level of experience and help supplement your education and training sections. And it was free!

The USMAP certificate is widely recognized. Participating in programs such as this can help you demonstrate to command your eagerness to learn and improve your skills. Proving your skills with a completed apprenticeship may help give you a leg up during your civilian job hunting.

If you would like more information on apprenticeships, check the DOL's website (http://www.doleta.gov/oa/). The direct link to the DOL USMAP site is http://www.doleta.gov/OA/usmap.cfm.

If you still need more motivation. . . . In 2012, the DOL published the results of a study designed to determine the benefits of participating in a registered apprenticeship (RA; see http://wdr.doleta.gov/research/FullText_Documents/ETAOP_2012_10.pdf). The study demonstrated that individuals who had participated in an RA program earned higher wages than those who did not. According to the study, "Over a career, the estimated earnings of RA participants earn an average of $98,718 more than similar nonparticipants."[2]

Chapter Twelve

Army and Navy Credentialing Opportunities On-Line (COOL)

The Army and Navy COOL are websites designed to assist service members in tailoring their education and/or career pathways based upon their Military Occupational Specialty (MOS) or rate. While the Marine Corps does not have its own COOL website, Marines may use either of the other branches' COOL websites to search for potential career growth opportunities.

ARMY AND NAVY COOL

http://www.cool.army.mil
http://www.cool.navy.mil

The Army and Navy COOL enable soldiers and sailors to find certifications and licenses associated with their MOSs or rates. If used properly, COOL may help some service members attain the civilian requirements related to their military specialty, thereby fast-tracking their pathway into a future career. Marines can use these websites for information pertaining to their MOSs as well. Each MOS or rate is translated on the Army and Navy COOL websites, making it easy for Marines to find their equivalent specialties.

The COOL websites allow users to search their military specialties for the civilian requirements and obtain information on licensure and certification, including test locations, payment possibilities, and resources to help prepare for exams. Sometimes exams are approved for GI Bill funding. If so, the website will indicate if it is possible once an MOS or rate has been selected and credentials are listed. The site will also demonstrate the program's accreditation, potential for college credit, and potential for promotion bonus points.

Review the list of icons found on the "Resource Icon Overview" tab located under the "COOL Overview" tab before researching your MOS or rate. That way, you will have a better understanding of the resources available to you under your specialty.

On the main page of the Army or Navy COOL site, select either an enlisted or officer search, and find your specialty. For example, under the Army COOL site, I selected the Warrant Officer MOS of 890A Ammunition Technician, and then selected 89D-Explosive Ordnance Disposal Specialist. The search results demonstrate numerous certification and licensing options related to the selected MOS. Options that lead to promotion points (only for that specific branch) are also listed here. Careful review of each selection will help service members determine which choices are most viable for personal career needs.

Choosing the "State Licenses" tab outlines the credentials a service member would need based upon state requirements. The "Apprenticeships" tab gives the user information pertaining to general overall understanding of apprenticeships, links to state-specific programs, and a master list of current occupations that have apprenticeship training available.

If you are following along on the sites, you will notice that the "Related Occupational Opportunities" and "Continuing Education" options are listed at the bottom of the page. Searching under "Related Occupational Opportunities," you will find lists of civilian and federal job titles, salaries, and a job search link. Links for the career possibilities take users to the O*NET Resource Center's "My Next Move for Veterans" (http://www.onetcenter.org/veterans.html), where service members can conduct career exploration. Lastly, searching under the "Continuing Education" link provides details of further career enhancement prospects; these are often in higher education.

The population of service members I counsel are mainly in infantry MOSs. Most of the websites available for MOS-related career exploration do not have many, if any, options listed under an 03MOS. The Army COOL website works wonders on infantry MOSs. All sorts of MOS career-related information can be found that is all applicable to infantry Marines. Spend some time on the website researching the different certifications and licenses to determine what is most relevant in your preferred field.

Further career-credentialing research can be conducted on the following websites:

Career One Stop: www.careeronestop.org/credentialing/Credentialing HomeReadMore.asp

Bureau of Labor Statistics: www.bls.gov/ooh/

Chapter Thirteen

VA Programs

The VA has several little-known programs available for veterans. The following three programs are ones I reference often during my counseling appointments. Always check your eligibility because many stipulations apply, such as the disability rating for vocational rehabilitation.

- Vocational Rehabilitation
- Work-Study Program
- GI Bill Tutorial Assistance

VOCATIONAL REHABILITATION

http://www.benefits.va.gov/vocrehab/index.asp

VA Vocational Rehabilitation (Voc Rehab) may assist service-connected veterans with job training, job skills, education, or employment accommodations. Voc Rehab counselors will work with individuals to determine career interests, skills, and existing abilities. They will help participants find jobs, on-the-job training, or apprenticeship programs. Formal education through an institution of higher learning might also be a necessary component to the retraining program. Veterans with severe disabilities can seek assistance through Voc Rehab to find help for independent living.

Eligible service members must meet the following parameters:

• If still on active duty: must be expecting to receive an honorable discharge, becoming service connected at a minimum of 20 percent.
• Veterans must receive a discharge that is anything other than dishonorable, and receive a VA service-connected rating of 10 percent or higher or a memorandum rating of 20 percent or higher.

After a veteran receives a service-connected rating, he or she must apply for Voc Rehab and schedule an appointment with a counselor. The vocational rehabilitation counselors (VRCs) will then complete an evaluation to determine final eligibility. If eligible, the VRC and the veteran will work together to determine the appropriate retraining pathway for the desired career outcome.

To apply for Voc Rehab, visit the VONAPP website (under the "Apply for Benefits" tab) on eBenefits and fill out Vocational Rehabilitation Form 28-1900.

eBenefits: https://www.ebenefits.va.gov/ebenefits-portal/ebenefits.portal

WORK-STUDY PROGRAM

VA's work-study program is a part-time option available to veterans who currently attend school at the three-quarter pursuit rate or higher. The program offers an opportunity for veteran students to earn money while pursuing education. Work-study payments are tax free. Participants work within a community of peers and build skills for résumés. All services rendered within the program relate to work within the VA. Eligible participants may not exceed 750 hours of work-study time per fiscal year.

Selected participants receive the federal minimum wage or state minimum wage, depending on which one is greater. Sometimes positions at colleges or universities are paid an extra amount by the school to make up the difference in pay between the institution and the VA work-study program.

Students are placed in a variety of positions depending upon availability, institution of attendance, and local VA facilities, such as Department of Veterans Affairs (DVA) regional offices or DVA medical offices. Priority may be given to veterans who have disability ratings of 30 percent or higher. Selection depends on factors such as job availability and a student's ability to complete the contract prior to exhausting his or her education benefits. Positions can include processing VA documents, assisting in VA information dispersal at educational institutions, and working at a local VA facility.

Veterans must be using one of the following programs in order to be eligible:

- Post 9/11 (including dependents using transferred entitlement)
- Montgomery GI Bill (MGIB) active or reserve
- Raising the Educational Achievement of Paraprofessionals (REAP) participants
- Post–Vietnam Era Veterans' Educational Assistance Program
- Dependents' Educational Assistance Program
- Dependents who are eligible under Chapter 35 (these may participate only while training in a state)
- Vocational Rehabilitation participants

To apply for a work-study allowance, visit the following VA link:

http://www.vba.va.gov/pubs/forms/VBA-22-8691-ARE.pdf

Or check with your local processing center:

http://www.gibill.va.gov/contact/regional_offices/index.html

GI BILL TUTORIAL ASSISTANCE

If you are a veteran and find that you are having trouble in one of your classes, tutorial assistance is available under MGIB and Post 9/11. Veterans eligible for this assistance have a deficiency in a subject or prerequisite subject that is required for his or her degree plan. The assistance is a supplement to your selected GI Bill. To be eligible, you must be pursuing education at a 50 percent or greater rate, have a deficiency, and be enrolled in the class during the term in which you are pursuing tutoring.

The cost cannot exceed $100 per month, or it cannot exceed the cost of the tutoring if less than $100. If the eligible student is under MGIB, there is no charge to the entitlement for the first $600 of tutoring received. If the eligible student elected the Post 9/11 GI Bill, there is no entitlement charge.

VA Form 22-1990t, "Application and Enrollment Certification for Individualized Tutorial Assistance," must be completed by the eligible student, the tutor, and the VA certifying official to apply for the benefit. The form must be signed, dated, and filled out either monthly or after a combination of months.

More information can be found on the VA website:

http://www.benefits.va.gov/gibill/tutorial_assistance.asp

Application and enrollment certification for individualized tutorial assistance:

http://www.vba.va.gov/pubs/forms/VBA-22-1990t-ARE.pdf

Chapter Fourteen

Random Service Member and Spousal-Based Programs and Organizations

Many programs are available for veterans and dependents to assist in education and career development. Some of the programs are volunteer based, and others are run on set schedules through institutions of higher learning. I have had several Marines go through the programs listed in this chapter. All speak highly of their experiences.

- Programs available for active-duty service members, veterans, and dependents
- Military Spouse Career Advancement Accounts (MyCAA)
- General advice for spouses

PROGRAMS AVAILABLE TO ACTIVE-DUTY SERVICE
MEMBERS, VETERANS, AND DEPENDENTS

I have run across a few organizations and programs the Marines have found
especially beneficial over the past few years. I am sure there are many more
wonderful programs available, but these are the few I use almost daily.
Usually, we discuss the organizations that have been around for a while, such
as the Veterans of Foreign Wars (VFW), Disabled American Veterans
(DAV), and American Veterans (AmVets), mainly because the organizations
have very established, credible programs.

Volunteering is a great way for veterans to continue to serve after they
leave the service and build skills for their résumés. Staying active with others
in the community can give veterans a sense of purpose. Marines are diehard
in their devotion to serve. I know one who actively participates with Habitat
for Humanity on weekends even though he is in a demanding instructor billet
with Infantry Training Battalion West, attends school, and has a family.

Younger Marines tend to prefer some of the newer organizations that
have come about more recently. Mostly, they cater more specifically to Iraq
and Afghanistan veterans, such as Iraq and Afghanistan Veterans of America
(IAVA). Team Rubicon and The Mission Continues are interesting possibilities for those interested in very hands-on participation; the programs handle
disaster relief and community building.

The first few organizations listed in this section offer services and programs for veterans. The last few are volunteer-based organizations.

Syracuse University Institute for Veterans and Military Families (IVMF)
http://vets.syr.edu/
Syracuse University, partnered with JPMorgan Chase & Co., has several
programs available through the IVMF to assist transitioning Post 9/11 service
members with future career plans depending upon their interests and pursuits. Many of the programs consist of free online courses that users can
access from any location at any time to promote veteran preparedness and
understanding of the civilian sector. Other courses are offered in a face-to-
face format that lasts roughly two weeks, and they are now available in
several different locations. IVMF offers courses for veterans, active-duty
service members, active-duty spouses, and disabled veterans.

The programs currently offered by IVMF include the following:

- EBV: Entrepreneurship Bootcamp for Veterans with Disabilities
- EBV-F: Entrepreneurship Bootcamp for Veterans' Families (caregivers and family members)
- V-WISE: Veteran Women Igniting the Spirit of Entrepreneurship for veteran women, female active-duty service members, and female family members
- E&G: Operation Endure & Grow for guard and reserve members and family
- B2B: Operation Boots to Business: From Service to Startup for transitioning service members
- Veterans' Career Transition Program (VCTP): Great program for active-duty service members to gain industry-level certificates in high-demand career fields.

Entrepreneurship Bootcamp for Veterans with Disabilities (EBV)
http://whitman.syr.edu/ebv/
EBV is designed to help veterans with service-connected disabilities in the entrepreneurship and small business management fields. Syracuse University, Texas A&M, Purdue University, UCLA, University of Connecticut, Louisiana State University, Florida State University, and Cornell University currently participate in EBV. EBV promotes long-term success for qualified veterans by teaching them how to create and sustain their entrepreneurial ventures (http://whitman.syr.edu/ebv/). All costs associated with EBV are covered by the program, including travel and lodging.

Entrepreneurship Bootcamp (EBV-F)
http://whitman.syr.edu/ebv/programs/families/
Entrepreneurship Bootcamp for Veterans' Families is offered through Syracuse University's Whitman School of Management and the Florida State University College of Business. The cost-free (including travel and lodging), one-week program assists family members in their pursuit to launch and maintain small businesses.

Eligible spouses include the following:

- A spouse, parent, sibling, or adult child who has a role supporting the veteran (health, education, work, etc.)
- A surviving spouse or adult child of a service member who died while serving after September 11, 2001

- An active-duty service member's spouse

V-Wise

http://whitman.syr.edu/vwise/

Veteran Women Igniting the Spirit of Entrepreneurship is a joint venture with the U.S. Small Business Administration (SBA). The program aims to help female veterans along the entrepreneurship and small business pathway by arming them with savvy business skills that enable them to turn business ideas into growing ventures. Business planning, marketing, accounting, operations, and human resources are covered within the tracks. The three-phase approach consists of a fifteen-day online course teaching the basic skills pertaining to being an entrepreneur, a three-day conference with two tracks for startups or those already in business, and delivery of a comprehensive listing packet that details the community-level resources available to participants.

Eligible participants are honorably separated female veterans from any branch of the military from any time period. Female spouses or partners of veteran business owners are eligible as well. Hotel rooms and taxes are covered, but other fees apply, such as travel.

Endure & Grow

http://apps.whitman.syr.edu/endureandgrow/

Operation Endure & Grow is a free online training program open to National Guard, reservists, and their family members. The program has two tracks: one for startups and the other for those who have been in business for over three years. The tracks are designed to assist participants in creating a new business and all related fundamentals, or to help an operating business stimulate growth.

Operation Boots to Business: From Service to Startup (B2B)

http://boots2business.org/

B2B is a partnership with the Syracuse University Whitman School of Business and the SBA. The program goal is to train transitioning service members to be business owners through three phases. Phases 1 and 2 are taken while the service member is still on active duty but is preparing to transition to the civilian world and attending the Transition Readiness Seminar (TRS). The third phase is accessible if veterans elect to continue and consists of an intensive instructor-led eight-week online "mini"-MBA.

Active-duty service members and their spouses or partners are eligible to participate in B2B during the separation process. The entire B2B program is free to participate in. Speak to your career planner about electing the Entrepreneurship Pathway during TRS.

Veterans' Career Transition Program (VCTP)
http://vets.syr.edu/education/employment-programs/
The VCTP offers numerous classes for career training and preparation. Many of the courses lead to high-demand industry-level certifications. This free online program is available to eligible post-9/11 veterans. The program is geared to help veterans understand corporate culture in the civilian business world. VCTP is a three-track program that includes Professional Skills, Tech, and Independent Study tracks.

The Professional Skills Track aims at training veterans in "soft" skills—mainly how to prepare for and implement job searches through conducting company research and creating cover letters and résumés. Foundations for advanced-level courses in Microsoft Office Word, Excel, PowerPoint, and Outlook can be achieved within this track. If a veteran participates in this track, he or she becomes an official Syracuse University student and receives a non-credit-based certificate upon completion.

The Tech Track is geared to prepare participants for careers in operations or information technology (IT). Industry-level certifications are offered in this level, and, where applicable, VCTP will cover exam fees. Participants also become Syracuse University students and receive non-credit-awarding certificates upon completion. Certificates include proficiency in subject areas such as Comp TIA (Server+, Network+, and A+), Oracle Database 11G, CCNA with CCENT certification, and Lean Six Sigma Green Belt.

The Independent Study Track hosts a large library of online coursework. Coursework include subject matter pertaining to professional and personal development, leadership, IT, and accounting and finance. Coursework is determined by veterans' demands and learning needs. Students will not be considered Syracuse University students.

American Corporate Partners (ACP)
http://www.acp-usa.org/
http://www.acp-advisornet.org
American Corporate Partners is a New York City–based national nonprofit organization founded in 2008 to help veterans transition from active duty

into the civilian workforce by enlisting the help of business professionals nationwide. Through mentoring, career counseling, and networking possibilities, ACP's goal is to build greater connections between corporate America and veteran communities. ACP has two available programs: ACP Advisor-Net, which is open to service members and their immediate family members, and a one-on-one Mentoring Program for post 9/11 veterans. ACP Advisor-Net is an online business community that offers veterans and immediate family members online career advice through Q&A discussions. The Mentoring Program connects employees from ACP's participating institutions with veterans or their spouses for mentoring options, networking assistance, and career development. More than fifty major companies are participating in ACP's mentoring program, and success stories and videos are available on ACP's website (http://www.acp-usa.org).

Hiring Our Heroes
http://www.uschamber.com/hiringourheroes
The U.S. Chamber of Commerce Foundation launched Hiring Our Heroes in 2011 to help veterans and spouses of active-duty service members find employment. The program works with state and local chambers as well as partners in the public, private, and nonprofit sectors. Hiring Our Heroes hosts career fairs aboard military bases. The program offers transition assistance, personal branding, and résumé workshops.

Google for Veterans and Families
http://www.googleforveterans.com/
Google offers a wide range of help for active-duty and veteran military members. They have tools to help families stay in touch during deployments, record military deployments, explore life after service (including résumé-building opportunities), and connect with other veterans.

Vet Net on Google+
http://www.vetnethq.com/
VetNet was launched by the U.S. Chamber of Commerce's Hiring Our Heroes program, the IVMF, and Hire Heroes USA as a partnership program. The program is set up similar to the TRS with different pathways designed to help transitioning service members find a more tailored approach to their specific needs. VetNet has three different pathways depending upon your goals: Basic Training, Career Connections, and Entrepreneur. The site hosts

live events and video seminars designed to provide information from those who have gone before them and to generate group discussions about civilian career and entrepreneur challenges. You can find many VetNet videos on YouTube.

Iraq and Afghanistan Veterans of America (IAVA)
http://iava.org/

IAVA offers service members another way to maintain the brotherhood while actively participating in an organization that promotes veteran well-being. The nonprofit and nonpartisan organization is strictly for veterans of the Iraq and Afghanistan campaigns. IAVA actively generates support for veteran-based policies at the local and federal levels while providing assistance to members through programs related to health, employment, education, and community resources. Their aim is to empower veterans who will be future leaders in our communities.

IAVA sponsors several academic and career-related programs for its members. Many of the Marines I work with have sought out IAVA for assistance in some manner. One active-duty gunnery sergeant I worked with was accepted to the Culinary Command program offered through IAVA's Rucksack. Culinary Command is a six-week, intensive, top-tier culinary arts program in New York with all costs covered, including travel and accommodations. Many other interesting programs are available for participation, including the War Writer's Campaign (my personal favorite). Programs are offered for online or on-the-ground participation depending upon members' needs.

The Mission Continues
http://missioncontinues.org/

The Mission Continues promotes community service and brotherhood through fellowships with local nonprofit organizations. The program empowers veterans to achieve postfellowship full-time employment or pursuit of higher education, while continuing a relationship with public service. Fellowships last for six months at twenty hours per week, and fellows receive a living stipend. The program also aims to bridge the military-civilian divide and allow veterans to connect with the community and feel a sense of belonging.

Team Rubicon

http://teamrubiconusa.org/

Team Rubicon unites veterans in a shared sense of purpose through disaster relief assistance by using the skills they have learned in the military. Volunteering veterans reintegrate into society and give back to communities in desperate need. Veterans are the perfect group of trained individuals to cope with the destruction seen in many places hit by natural disasters. Team Rubicon uses the combat skills that many veterans have already cultivated to facilitate greater momentum during disaster relief operations. Many of the circumstances faced during disasters are similar to the conditions that service members have already been trained to handle while on active duty.

The Veterans Posse Foundation

http://www.possefoundation.org/veterans-posse-program

The Veterans Posse Program aims to support veterans who are interested in attending bachelor's degree programs at prestigious institutions across the country. The program creates cohorts of veterans and prepares them to matriculate into select schools. For example, the Veterans Posse Program is currently looking for twenty veterans who are interested in Vassar College or Wesleyan University. Selectees will attend a one-month-long, all-inclusive, pre-collegiate summer training program in New York City designed to foster leadership and academic excellence. Vassar and Wesleyan guarantee that selectees' full tuition will be covered even after GI Bill and the Yellow Ribbon Program funding runs out.

Warrior-Scholar Project

http://www.warrior-scholar.org

The Warrior-Scholar Project is a two-week intensive program designed to promote veteran academic success. Through classes, workshops, discussions, and one-on-one tutoring sessions, veterans are taught how to transition into higher education, challenged to become leaders in their classes at their institutions, and prepared to overcome challenges and embrace new learning experiences. Yale, Harvard, and the University of Michigan host the program. Be aware that there is some cost involved with this program.

Student Veterans of America (SVA)

http://www.studentveterans.org/

The SVA organization is a nonprofit designed to help veterans succeed in higher education. Groups of student veterans on school campuses across the country have gotten together to create member chapters. The goal of these chapters is to help veterans acculturate to college life by offering peer-to-peer support. Chapters organize activities and offer networking opportunities. SVA develops partnerships with other organizations that also aim to promote veteran academic success. Through these partnerships, the SVA has helped to create several new scholarship opportunities. Check their website for more information.

MILITARY SPOUSE CAREER ADVANCEMENT ACCOUNTS (MYCAA)

https://aiportal.acc.af.mil/mycaa

Military One Source facilitates the MyCAA program. The program offers $4,000 to eligible spouses of active-duty military members to be used for education, whether traditional or nontraditional in nature. MyCAA is good for an associate degree, a certification, or a license.

The program cannot be used toward a bachelor's degree, but it can also be used for programs after a spouse receives a bachelor's degree. For example, I used the program for a supplementary teaching credential offered through the University of California, San Diego, after completing a master's degree in education when I qualified through my husband's rank.

MyCAA aims to increase the portable career skills of active-duty service members' spouses by developing their professional credentials to help them find and maintain work. Military One Source counselors can help eligible spouses find specific programs or schools that participate in the program. Counselors can also aid spouses in identifying local sources of assistance, such as state and local financial assistance, transportation, and child care. In addition, they can assist with employment referrals.

Eligible spouses must be married to active-duty service members in the following ranks:

- E1–E5
- O1–O2
- WO1–CWO2

MyCAA will *NOT* cover the following:

- Prior courses
- Books, supplies, student activities, and the like
- Prepayment deposits
- Audited courses or internships
- Nonacademic or ungraded courses
- Courses taken more than one time
- College-Level Examination Program (CLEP) or DSST exams
- Associate of arts degrees in general studies or liberal arts
- Personal enrichment courses
- Transportation, lodging, and child care
- Course extensions
- Study abroad

To apply, visit https://aiportal.acc.af.mil/mycaa or call (800) 342-9647 to speak with a Military One Source Counselor.

GENERAL ADVICE FOR SPOUSES

Unfortunately, besides MyCAA, there is no other direct financial assistance for spouses to pursue their educations. If spouses are just beginning their educations and willing to attend the local community college, MyCAA will typically cover an associate degree, depending upon the cost of the school. Many community colleges offer associate degrees fully online, which may also offer spouses with children more flexibility.

Past the associate degree, scholarship options (see the "Scholarship" section in chapter 6) and in a few cases transferring GI Bill benefits from the active-duty spouse are the best bets. Many universities and colleges offer tuition discounts to spouses of active-duty service members but usually not enough to fully alleviate the financial burden.

Spouses should also apply for Federal Student Aid through the Free Application for Federal Student Aid (FAFSA). More information on Federal Student Aid can be found in chapter 6, "Cost and Payment Resources." Many spouses receive all or a portion of the Pell Grant money (see the "Federal Student Aid" section), which does not need to be paid back.

Spouses are entitled to receive the in-state tuition rates at state schools in whatever state they are stationed with their active-duty service member. The

Higher Education Opportunity Act (H.R. 4137) signed into law on August 14, 2008, guarantees this benefit. This law eliminates all out-of-state tuition fees and at least helps to ease the financial burden of pursuing higher education. Be aware that many schools will want to see a copy of the service members' orders to verify in-state tuition.

Some states offer low-income tuition waivers to residents usually through the state-based community colleges. Because spouses are eligible for in-state tuition (so are active-duty members!), they may be eligible for this type of waiver as well.

For instance, California offers the Board of Governor's Fee Waiver (see http://home.cccapply.org/money/bog-fee-waiver) through the state community colleges. Many spouses stationed in California with their active-duty service member spouses are attending community colleges in California and receiving this waiver, and they do not pay to attend school. In fact, many Marines receive this waiver as well and are not bound by the rules of Tuition Assistance.

Always check with the local community colleges first if you are a spouse and are just getting started. In most cases, it is hard to beat their low tuition rates and the flexible class offerings. Community colleges typically also offer vocational programs at drastically reduced prices when compared to private institutions. They should be your number-one starting point!

The Officers' Wives' Clubs aboard the different bases offer scholarships for enlisted Marine Corps dependents. If you can write an essay and watch the deadline dates, that is usually a decent option for a funding source. As a last resort, you may want to discuss GI Bill transferability with an education counselor aboard your base. Just remember, if you go that route, that those are benefits that your active-duty spouse will not have at a later date. For more information regarding eligibility and the process to transfer the GI Bill, see chapter 6, "Cost and Payment Resources."

Transferring the GI Bill to a spouse so that he or she can use it while the service member is on active duty is not my first goal in most cases. Spouses are not eligible for the housing stipend while the Marine is still actively serving, but children are eligible. Let's consider the following case.

A Marine transfers his GI Bill to his spouse while still on active duty. She uses the benefit to attend California State University, San Marcos (CSUSM). While she will receive the book stipend, she will not receive the housing allowance. Her school is paid for, and she has some extra money for books.

Another Marine transfers his GI Bill to his daughter. His daughter attends the same institution and receives the book stipend as well as the housing stipend, which is currently sitting at $2,052 per month. At the end of a nine-month school year, the monthly stipend totals $18,468. That is also the amount of money the spouse did not get while using the benefit. Now consider the same monthly amount (even though it receives cost-of-living adjustments) over a four-year bachelor's degree: $73,872.

For this reason, only in very few circumstances do I recommend spouses using transferred GI Bill benefits while the Marine is still on active duty. Obviously, this does not take into account different variables. For example, maybe the couple does not plan on having children, maybe the Marine has attained the maximum level of education he or she is interested in pursuing, or maybe the children are very young and there are no other resources for the spouse. In the end, the decision becomes personal and all outlets must be pursued.

Appendix 1

Websites

ACCREDITING BODIES

Middle States Association of Colleges and Schools: http://www.msche.org/

New England Association of School and Colleges: http://cihe.neasc.org/

North Central Association of Colleges and Schools: http://www.ncahlc.org/

Northwest Commission on Colleges and Universities: http://www.nwccu.org/

Southern Association of Colleges and Schools: http://www.sacscoc.org/

WASC Senior College and University Commission: http://www.wascweb.org/

RESOURCE WEBSITES

ACT: http://www.act.org

American Corporate Partners (ACP): http://www.acp-usa.org/, www.acp-advisornet.org

American Council on Education: http://www.acenet.edu

American Psychological Association (APA): http://www.apa.org

Army COOL: http://www.cool.army.mil

Board of Governors Waiver, California: http://www.icanaffordcollege. com/?navId=10

Bureau of Labor Statistics: www.bls.gov/ooh/

California Board of Governors Waiver: http://home.cccapply.org/money/ bog-fee-waiver

Career One Stop: www.careeronestop.org/credentialing/Credentialing HomeReadMore.asp

CareerScope: www.gibill.va.gov/studenttools/careerscope/index.html

Cash for College: http://www.calgrants.org/index.cfm?navid=16

College Navigator: http://nces.ed.gov/collegenavigator/

Council for Higher Education Accreditation (CHEA): http://www.chea. org/search/default.asp

DANTES Kuder: http://www.dantes.kuder.com

Defense Language Institute Foreign Language Center (DLIFLC): http:// www.dliflc.edu

eKnowledge Corporation & NFL Players: http://www.eknowledge.com/ military

Expeditionary Warfare School and Command and Staff: https://www. tecom.usmc.mil/cdet/sitepages/masters_credit.aspx

Federal Student Aid: http://www.fafsa.ed.gov/

GI Bill information: http://www.gibill.va.gov

Google for Veterans and Families: http://www.googleforveterans.com

Grammar Book: http://www.grammarbook.com

Grammar Bytes: http://www.chompchomp.com

Guide to Grammar Writing: http://grammar.ccc.commnet.edu/grammar/

Hiring Our Heroes: http://www.uschamber.com/hiringourheroes

Institutional Accreditation Search: www.ope.ed.gov/accreditation/, www. chea.org/search/default.asp, http://nces.ed.gov/collegenavigator/

Iraq and Afghanistan Veterans of America (IAVA): http://iava.org/

Joint Services Transcript: https://jst.doded.mil/

Khan Academy: http://www.khanacademy.org

Know Before You Enroll: http://www.knowbeforeyouenroll.org

Make the Connection: http://maketheconnection.net/

Midwest Student Exchange Program: http://msep.mhec.org/

Military Spouse Career Advancement Accounts (MyCAA): https:// aiportal.acc.af.mil/mycaa

Mission Continues: http://missioncontinues.org/

My Next Move for Veterans: http://www.mynextmove.org/vets/

National Association of Credential Evaluation Services: http://www.naces.org/

Navy COOL: http://www.cool.navy.mil

O*NET OnLine: http://www.onetonline.org/

Petersons: http://www.petersons.com/dod

Purdue Owl: http://owl.english.purdue.edu/owl/

Purple Math: http://www.purplemath.com

SAT: http://www.collegeboard.org

States' Departments of Veterans Affairs Offices: http://www.va.gov/statedva.htm

State workforce agencies: http://www.servicelocator.org/OWSLinks.asp

Student Veterans of America: http://www.studentveterans.org

Student Veterans of America In-State Tuition Map: http://www.studentveterans.org/what-we-do/in-state-tuition.html

Syracuse University Institute for Veterans and Military Families (IVMF): http://vets.syr.edu/

Team Rubicon: http://teamrubiconusa.org/

University of San Diego's Veterans' Legal Clinic: http://www.sandiego.edu/veteransclinic/

U.S. Department of Defense Memorandum of Understanding: http://www.dodmou.com

U.S. Department of Education College Affordability and Transparency Center: http://collegecost.ed.gov/

U.S. Department of Education—national accrediting agencies: http://ope.ed.gov/accreditation/

U.S. Department of Labor apprenticeship information: http://www.doleta.gov/oa/

U.S. Department of Labor's career search tool: http://www.mynextmove.org/

U.S. Department of Labor unemployment information: http://workforcesecurity.doleta.gov/unemploy/uifactsheet.asp

U.S. Department of Veterans Affairs (VA): http://www.va.gov

U.S. Military Apprenticeship Program (USMAP): https://usmap.cnet.navy.mil

VA Chapter 36 educational support counseling: http://www.gibill.va.gov/support/counseling_services/

VA Vet Centers: http://www.vetcenter.va.gov/index.asp

VA Vocational Rehabilitation: http://www.benefits.va.gov/vocrehab/index.asp

VA Work Study Local Office Search: http://www.gibill.va.gov/contact/regional_offices/index.html

VA Yellow Ribbon Program: http://www.gibill.va.gov/benefits/post_911_gibill/yellow_ribbon_program.html

Vet Net on Google+: http://www.vetnethq.com/

Veterans On-Line Application (VONAPP): http://vabenefits.vba.va.gov/vonapp/

Veterans Posse Foundation: http://www.possefoundation.org/veterans-posse-program

Veterans Upward Bound: http://www.navub.org/

Warrior-Scholar Project: http://www.warrior-scholar.org

APA FORMAT GUIDANCE

American Psychological Association: http://www.apastyle.org
Purdue Owl: https://owl.english.purdue.edu/owl/resource/560/01/

CITATION FORMATTING

Citation Machine: http://citationmachine.net/index2.php
KnightCite: https://www.calvin.edu/library/knightcite/

MLA FORMAT GUIDANCE

California State University, Los Angeles: http://web.calstatela.edu/library/guides/3mla.pdf

Cornell University Library: www.library.cornell.edu/resrch/citmanage/mla

Purdue Owl: https://owl.english.purdue.edu/owl/resource/747/01/

STATES CURRENTLY WITH IN-STATE TUITION LEGISLATION

Alabama: http://openstates.org/al/bills/2013rs/HB424/documents/ALD00016731/

Arizona: http://dvs.az.gov/tuition.aspx

California: http://www.calvet.ca.gov/VetServices/Education.aspx

Colorado: http://highered.colorado.gov/Finance/Residency/requirements. html

Florida: http://www.flsenate.gov/Session/Bill/2014/7015/BillText/er/PDF

Idaho: http://www.legislature.idaho.gov/legislation/2010/S1367.pdf

Illinois: http://www2.illinois.gov/veterans/benefits/pages/education.aspx

Indiana: http://www.in.gov/legislative/bills/2013/SE/SE0177.1.html

Kentucky: http://cpe.ky.gov/policies/academicpolicies/residency.htm

Louisiana: http://legiscan.com/LA/text/HB435/id/649958

Maine: http://www.mainelegislature.org/legis/bills/getDoc.asp?id=39934

Maryland: http://mgaleg.maryland.gov/webmga/frmStatutesText.aspx? article=ged&section=15-106.4&ext=html&session=2014RS&tab= subject5

Minnesota: https://www.revisor.mn.gov/statutes/?id=197.775&format= pdf

Missouri: http://www.senate.mo.gov/13info/BTS_Web/Bill.aspx?Session Type=R&BillID=17138567

Nebraska: http://nebraskalegislature.gov/FloorDocs/Current/PDF/Final/ LB740.pdf

Nevada: http://leg.state.nv.us/Session/77th2013/Bills/AB/AB260_EN.pdf

New Mexico: http://www.dvs.state.nm.us/benefits.html

North Dakota: www.legis.nd.gov/cencode/t15c10.pdf?20131106152541

Ohio: http://veteransaffairs.ohio.gov/

Oregon: https://olis.leg.state.or.us/liz/2013R1/Measures/Text/HB2158/ Enrolled

South Dakota: http://legis.state.sd.us/statutes/DisplayStatute.aspx?Type= Statute&Statute=13-53-29.1

Tennessee: http://www.capitol.tn.gov/Bills/108/Bill/SB1433.pdf

Texas: http://www.statutes.legis.state.tx.us/Docs/ED/htm/ED.54.htm#54. 241

Utah: http://le.utah.gov/code/TITLE53B/pdf/53B08_010200.pdf

Virginia: http://lis.virginia.gov/cgi-bin/legp604.exe?000+cod+23-7.4

Washington: http://apps.leg.wa.gov/documents/billdocs/2013-14/Pdf/ Bills/Senate%20Passed%20Legislature/5318.PL.pdf

STATES CURRENTLY WITH STATE-BASED
EDUCATION BENEFITS

Alabama: http://www.va.state.al.us/scholarship.htm
California: http://www.calvet.ca.gov/VetServices/Education.aspx
Connecticut: http://www.ct.gov/ctva/cwp/view.asp?A=2014&Q=290874
Florida: http://floridavets.org/?page_id=60
Illinois: http://www2.illinois.gov/veterans/benefits/Pages/education.aspx
Indiana: http://www.in.gov/dva/2378.htm
Maryland: http://www.mdva.state.md.us/state/scholarships.html
Massachusetts: www.mass.gov/veterans/education/financial-assistance/
tuition-waivers.html
Minnesota: http://mn.gov/mdva/resources/education/minnesotagibill.jsp
Missouri: http://www.dhe.mo.gov/files/moretheroesact.pdf
Montana: http://data.opi.mt.gov/bills/mca/20/25/20-25-421.htm
New York: http://veterans.ny.gov/state-benefits.html
North Carolina: http://www.doa.state.nc.us/vets/scholarshipclasses.aspx
Oregon: www.oregon.gov/odva/BENEFITS/Pages/OregonEducation
Benefit.aspx
Puerto Rico: http://www.nasdva.com/puertorico.html
South Carolina: www.govoepp.state.sc.us/va/benefits.html#ed_assis
South Dakota: http://mva.sd.gov/vet_benefits_info.html#Free+Tuition+
for+Veterans
Tennessee: http://www.tn.gov/sos/rules/1640/1640-01-22.20090529.pdf
Texas: http://veterans.portal.texas.gov/en/Pages/education.aspx
Utah: http://veterans.utah.gov/homepage/stateBenefits/
Virgin Islands: http://www.militaryvi.org/benefits/
Washington State: http://apps.leg.wa.gov/RCW/default.aspx?cite=28B.
15.621
West Virginia: http://www.veterans.wv.gov/Pages/default.aspx
Wisconsin: http://www.wisvets.com/wisgibill
Wyoming: www.communitycolleges.wy.edu/Data/Sites/1/commission
Files/Programs/Veteran/_doc/statue-19-14-106.pdf

Appendix 2

Commonly Used Acronyms

AA: associate of arts

AAS: associate of applied science

BA: bachelor of arts

BOG Fee Waiver: Board of Governors Fee Waiver

BS: bachelor of science

CC: community college

CHEA: Council for Higher Education Accreditation

COE: certificate of eligibility

EAS: end of active service

FAFSA: Free Application for Federal Student Aid

FSA: Federal Student Aid

FY: fiscal year

GPA: grade point average

IAVA: Iraq and Afghanistan Veterans of America

JST: Joint Services Transcript

MA: master of arts

MASP: Military Academic Skills Program

MD: medical doctor

MGIB: Montgomery GI Bill

MOS: Military Occupational Specialty

MS: master of science

MSEP: Midwest Student Exchange Program

OJT: on-the-job training
PCS: permanent change of station
PhD: doctor of philosophy
SOC: Servicemembers Opportunity Colleges
SOCMAR: Servicemembers Opportunity Colleges Marine Corps Agreement
SVA: Student Veterans of America
TA: tuition assistance
TAD: temporary additional duty
TAP: Transition Assistance Program
VA: Veterans Administration
VET REPS: veterans representatives
VONAPP: Veterans On-Line Application
VOTECH: vocational technical
YRP: Yellow Ribbon Program

Appendix 3

Education Center Contact Information

Henderson Hall, Virginia
(703) 614-9104
http://www.mccshh.com/learning.html

Marine Corps Air Ground Combat Center (MCAGCC) Twenty-Nine Palms,
California
(760) 830-6881
http://www.mccs29palms.com/pages/mfamservices/education.html

Marine Corps Air Station (MCAS) Cherry Point, North Carolina
(252) 466-2046/3500
http://www.mccscherrypoint.com/education.asp

MCAS Miramar, California
(858) 577-1801
http://www.mccsmiramar.com/education_center.html

MCAS New River, North Carolina
(910) 449-6623/5397/6233
http://www.mccsnr.com/education.html

MCAS Yuma, Arizona
(928) 269-3589
http://www.yuma.usmc-mccs.org/index.cfm/military-family/lifelong-learning/

Marine Corps Base (MCB) Camp Lejeune, North Carolina
(910) 451-3091/9127
http://www.mccslejeune.com/EDU/

MCB Camp Pendleton, California
(760) 725-6414/6660
http://www.mccscp.com/jec

MCB Hawaii
(808) 257-2158
http://mccshawaii.com/edcenter/

MCB Okinawa, Japan
Education@okinawa.usmc-mccs.org
http://www.mccsokinawa.com/educationandcareerservices/

MCB Quantico, Virginia
(703) 784-3340
http://www.quantico.usmc-mccs.org/index.cfm/marine-family-programs/voluntary-education-center/

Marine Corps Logistics Base (MCLB) Albany, Georgia
(229) 639-5276
http://www.marineandfamilyservices.com/baseeducation/

MCLB Barstow, California
(760) 577-6018
http://www.mccsbarstow.com/education/

Marine Corps Recruit Depot (MCRD) Beaufort, South Carolina
(843) 228-7474
http://www.mccs-sc.com/lifelong/index.asp

MCRD Parris Island, South Carolina
(843) 228-2086
http://www.mccs-sc.com/lifelong/index.asp

MCRD San Diego, California
(619) 524-1275
http://www.mccsmcrd.com/personalandprofessionaldevelopment/
educationcenter/index.html

Notes

2. WHICH SCHOOL IS BEST FOR ME?

1. Kimberly Griffin and Claire Gilbert, Center for American Progress, "Easing the Transition from Combat to Classroom," last modified April 2012, accessed June 2, 2013, http://www.americanprogress.org/wp-content/uploads/issues/2012/04/pdf/student_veterans.pdf.

4. WHAT SHOULD I LOOK FOR IN A SCHOOL?

1. U.S. Senate, Health, Education, Labor, and Pensions Committee, "For Profit Higher Education: The Failure to Safeguard the Federal Investment and Ensure Student Success," last modified July 30, 2012, accessed April 14, 2014, http://www.help.senate.gov/imo/media/for_profit_report/Contents.pdf.

2. Sandy Baum and Jennifer Ma, College Board, "Trends in Higher Education 2012," accessed July 12, 2013, http://advocacy.collegeboard.org/sites/default/files/college-pricing-2012-full report_0.pdf.

3. National Association of Independent Colleges and Universities, "Independent Colleges and Universities: A National Profile," last modified March 8, 2011, accessed April 14, 2014, http://www.naicu.edu/docLib/20110317_NatProfile-Final4.pdf.

4. Judith Eaton, Council for Higher Education Accreditation, "An Overview of U.S. Accreditation," last modified August 2012, accessed April 14, 2014, http://www.chea.org/pdf/Overview%20of%20US%20Accreditation%202012.pdf.

5. Marine Corps Air Station Beaufort, "Go to College after the Marine Corps," last modified November 8, 2012, accessed April 14, 2014, http://www.beaufort.marines.mil/News/NewsView/tabid/14981/Article/133935/go-to-college-after-the-marine-corps.aspx.

7. PRIOR LEARNING CREDIT

1. American Council on Education, "Military Guide Frequently Asked Questions," accessed December 13, 2013, http://www.acenet.edu/news-room/Pages/Military-Guide-Frequently-Asked-Questions.aspx.

9. FREE SUBJECT MATTER STUDY SUPPORT

1. United States Department of Education, "Veterans Upward Bound Program," last modified September 27, 2013, accessed April 15, 2014, http://www2.ed.gov/programs/triovub/index.html.

11. ON-THE-JOB TRAINING AND APPRENTICESHIP PROGRAMS

1. U.S. Department of Labor, Employment and Training Administration, "Registered Apprenticeship: A Solution to the Skills Shortage," accessed February 2, 2014, http://www.doleta.gov/oa/pdf/fsfront.pdf.

2. U.S. Department of Labor, Employment and Training Administration, "Registered Apprenticeship: A Solution to the Skills Shortage."

Bibliography

American Council on Education, "Military Guide Frequently Asked Questions." Accessed December 13, 2013. http://www.acenet.edu/news-room/Pages/Military-Guide-Frequently-Asked-Questions.aspx

Baum, Sandy, and Jennifer Ma. College Board, "Trends in Higher Education 2012." Accessed July 12, 2013. http://advocacy.collegeboard.org/sites/default/files/college-pricing-2012-full report_0.pdf

College Board, "Veterans and College Admissions: FAQs." Accessed January 12, 2014. https://bigfuture.collegeboard.org/get-in/applying-101/veterans-college-admission-faqs

College Board, "Why Community College." Accessed January 11, 2014. http://professionals.collegeboard.com/guidance/college/community-college

Council for Higher Education Accreditation, "The Fundamentals of Accreditation." Last modified September 2002. Accessed February 10, 2014. http://www.academic.umn.edu/provost/reviews/gen_institutional/fund_accred_20ques_02.pdf

Council of Regional Accrediting Commissions, "Regional Accreditation and Student Learning: Principles for Good Practice." Last modified May 2003. Accessed April 14, 2014. http://www.msche.org/publications/Regnlsl050208135331.pdf

Defense Activity for Non-Traditional Education Support, "Troops to Teachers." Last modified July 2, 2013. Accessed April 14, 2014. http://www.dantes.doded.mil/index.html

Eaton, Judith. The Council for Higher Education Accreditation, "An Overview of U.S. Accreditation." Last modified August 2012. Accessed April 14, 2014. http://www.chea.org/pdf/Overview%20of%20US%20Accreditation%202012.pdf

Federal Trade Commission, "Choosing a Vocational School." Last modified August 2012. Accessed April 14, 2014. http://www.consumer.ftc.gov/articles/0241-choosing-vocational-school

Griffin, Kimberly, and Claire Gilbert. The Center for American Progress, "Easing the Transition from Combat to Classroom." Last modified April 2012. Accessed June 2, 2013. http://www.americanprogress.org/wp-content/uploads/issues/2012/04/pdf/student_veterans.pdf

Kleinman, Rebecca, Annalisa Mastri, Davin Reed, Debbie Reed, Samina Sattar, Albert Yung-Hsu Liu, and Jessica Ziegler. Mathematica Policy Research, "An Effectiveness Assessment and Cost-Benefit Analysis of Registered Apprenticeship in 10 States." Last modified July

25, 2012. Accessed April 14, 2014. http://wdr.doleta.gov/research/FullText_Documents/ETAOP_2012_10.pdf

Kurtzleben, Danielle. "Apprenticeships a Little-Traveled Path to Jobs." *U.S. News and World Report*, January 13, 2013. Accessed April 14, 2014. http://www.usnews.com/news/articles/2013/01/13/apprenticeships-a-little-traveled-path-to-jobs

Marine Corps Air Station Beaufort, "Go to College after the Marine Corps." Last modified November 8, 2012. Accessed April 14, 2014. http://www.beaufort.marines.mil/News/NewsView/tabid/14981/Article/133935/go-to-college-after-the-marine-corps.aspx

Maryland Higher Education Commission, "The Importance of Accreditation." Last modified November 14, 2011. Accessed April 14, 2014. http://www.mhec.state.md.us/highered/colleges_universities/accreditation.asp

National Association of Independent Colleges and Universities, "Independent Colleges and Universities: A National Profile." Last modified March 8, 2011. Accessed April 14, 2014. http://www.naicu.edu/docLib/20110317_NatProfile-Final4.pdf

National Skills Coalition, "On-the-Job Training Recommendations for Inclusion in a Federal Jobs Bill." Last modified January 2010. Accessed April 14, 2014. http://www.nationalskillscoalition.org/assets/reports-/nsc_issuebrief_ojt_2010-01.pdf

Peterson's, "Colleges and Universities: Choosing the Right Fit." Accessed June 3, 2013. http://www.petersons.com/college-search/colleges-universities-choosing-fit.aspx

State of California Employment Development Department, "Workforce Investment Act." Accessed January 23, 2014. www.edd.ca.gov/jobs_and_Training/Workforce_Investment_Act.htm

U.S. Department of Education, "Accreditation in the United States." Last modified February 12, 2014. Accessed April 14, 2014. http://www2.ed.gov/admins/finaid/accred/accreditation_pg2.html, http://professionals.collegeboard.com/guidance/college/community-college

U.S. Department of Education, "Career Colleges and Technical Schools: Choosing a School." Last modified June 18, 2013. Accessed April 14, 2014. http://www2.ed.gov/students/prep/college/consumerinfo/choosing.html

U.S. Department of Education, "Federal versus Private Loans." Accessed December 13, 2013. http://studentaid.ed.gov/types/loans/federal-vs-private

U.S. Department of Education, "Learn about Your College and Career School Options." Accessed May 15, 2013. http://studentaid.ed.gov/prepare-for-college/choosing-schools/types, http://www.help.senate.gov/imo/media/for_profit_report/PartI.pdf

U.S. Department of Education, "Veterans Upward Bound Program." Last modified September 27, 2013. Accessed April 14, 2014. http://www2.ed.gov/programs/triovub/index.html

U.S. Department of Labor. Employment and Training Administration, "Registered Apprenticeship: A Solution to the Skills Shortage." Accessed February 2, 2014. http://www.doleta.gov/oa/pdf/fsfront.pdf

U.S. Department of Labor, "Unemployment Compensation for Ex-Servicemembers." Accessed September 12, 2013. http://workforcesecurity.doleta.gov/unemploy/ucx.asp

U.S. Department of Labor, "Unemployment Insurance." Accessed September 12, 2013. http://www.dol.gov/dol/topic/unemployment-insurance/

U.S. Department of Veterans Affairs, "On-the-Job Training and Apprenticeship." Last modified December 3, 2013. Accessed February 18, 2014. http://www.benefits.va.gov/gibill/onthejob_apprenticeship.asp

U.S. Department of Veterans Affairs, "Tuition Assistance Top Up." Last modified December 5, 2013. Accessed April 14, 2014. http://www.benefits.va.gov/gibill/tuition_assistance.asp

U.S. Military Apprenticeship Program, "Program Information." Last modified October 31, 2013. Accessed April 14, 2014. https://usmap.cnet.navy.mil/usmapss/static/genInfo.jsp

U.S. Senate, Health, Education, Labor, and Pensions Committee, "For Profit Higher Education: The Failure to Safeguard the Federal Investment and Ensure Student Success." Last modified July 30, 2012. Accessed April 14, 2014. http://www.help.senate.gov/imo/media/for_profit_report/Contents.pdf

Index

About the Author

Jillian Ventrone is the wife of an active-duty infantry Marine, the sister-in-law of a reserve Marine, the daughter of an Air Force veteran, the granddaughter of an Army Air Corps/Air Force veteran, and the granddaughter of a soldier lost in World War II. She, her husband, and their daughter live in Southern California, where her husband is currently stationed. She is an avid writer who is passionate about veterans' higher education.